"*For a long time, the debate about Australia's past has been torn between a Left that says it was all too shameful and a Right that sometimes struggles to acknowledge that which was shameful. In this book, Dr Sherry Sufi has struck the balance just right. He argues that Australia is not a racist country built on stolen land and it certainly has a way of life worth defending. I agree with these conclusions. This book should be prescribed reading.*"

Warren Mundine – Indigenous Affairs Activist

I0023426

AUSTRALIA ON TRIAL
ACCUSATIONS AND DEFENCE

Sherry Sufi

Connor Court Publishing

Published by Connor Court Publishing Pty Ltd, 2024.

Copyright © Sherry Sufi, 2024.

ALL RIGHTS RESERVED.

This book contains material protected under International and Federal Copyright Laws and Treaties. Any unauthorised reprint or use of this material is prohibited. No part of this book may be reproduced or transmitted in any form or by any means, electronic or mechanical, including photocopying, recording, or by any information storage and retrieval system without express written permission from the publisher.

CONNOR COURT PUBLISHING PTY LTD
PO Box 7257
Redland Bay QLD 4165
sales@connorcourt.com
www.connorcourtpublishing.com.au

Disclaimer: The information presented in this book is based on the author's understanding of the subjects it seeks to tackle in a manner that is accessible to members of the general public. While every effort has been made to ensure accuracy, neither the author nor the publisher are liable for any inaccuracies, errors or omissions. This book is intended for educational purposes.

ISBN: 9781922815996

Cover design by Maria Giordano

Front cover picture: Painting by E. Phillips Fox depicting the landing of Lieutenant James Cook, RN, at Botany Bay, 29 April 1770, Public domain.

Printed in Australia.

"A robust, not to say muscular, defence of Australia against the fashionable claims that it's a racist country established on stolen land, with a chronic cultural cringe. Anyone who loves Australia will appreciate Sufi's rebuttal of such bunk."

Niall Ferguson — Author of 'Empire: How Britain Made the Modern World'.

"For a long time, the debate about Australia's past has been torn between a Left that says it was all too shameful and a Right that sometimes struggles to acknowledge that which was shameful. In this book, Dr Sherry Sufi has struck the balance just right. He argues that Australia is not a racist country built on stolen land and it certainly has a way of life worth defending. I agree with these conclusions. This book should be prescribed reading."

Warren Mundine — Indigenous Affairs Activist.

"In this book, Dr Sherry Sufi puts Australia to the test and rates us far more highly than the critics from the 'black armband' brigade. He shows quite persuasively that on balance, we have far more to celebrate than to lament about our great nation."

Tony Abbott — 28th Prime Minister of Australia.

"When a country forgets the breadth and depth of its history and achievements, it loses self belief in its cultural identity and hunger for future accomplishment. This book is a timely reminder of the meteoric rise of Australia as a developed nation and the great contribution made by Australians from all backgrounds and all walks of life. The insipid and intellectually vacuous notion of historic and systematic racism in Australia does not bear out in the fullness of the facts, nor does it fit with the continued popularity of Australia as a destination for migrants seeking freedom and opportunity. As a child of migrants, there is no other place I'd rather be".

Caroline Di Russo — Political Commentator.

"In plain but lucid language, Sherry Sufi takes on the Australian intellectual elite that has left the majority of the public in our suburban heartland uninformed about this country's major historical achievements in politics and justice. Australia On Trial is an impressive and informative answer to the most recent academic debates that warp our understanding and narrow our appreciation of the real Australia."

Keith Windschuttle — Editor-in-Chief, Quadrant.

"It is so refreshing to read a rational exploration of the foundation of this wonderful and in so many ways, trail-blazing nation. Dr Sherry Sufi has provided a real circuit-breaker in the cultural wars. He addresses the cultural amnesia in a calm and logical fashion. A must read for all who love our great country."

Piers Akerman — Author, Political Commentator and News Anchor.

"This book explodes myths. It uses the power of history and fact-checking to explode the myths of 'racist' Australia and 'living on stolen land.' Recent events have pushed race relations into an unhealthy place in this country—a place where they don't deserve to be. This book is the aspirin for that headache. Read it and you'll discover that the journey towards closed-minded prejudice is shaken to its core by the road humps of truth."

Kel Richards — Author, Journalist and Broadcaster.

"With a watchmaker's precision, Sufi pulls apart the accusations levelled by the left against this country and rebuts them clinically, one by one."

Rocco Loiacono — Legal Academic and Sky News Contributor.

"As some Australian commentators continue to denigrate Australia's history we have Dr Sherry Sufi bursting into print with an easy to read book analysing their arguments and firmly settling on the inescapable conclusion that Australia is neither stolen land nor racist. Dr Sufi both elegantly, and persuasively deconstructs the assertions which unchallenged would be an existential threat for Australia and her future. Relying on numerous verifiable Australian characteristics the case for an Australia for which we can all be thankful is strongly presented by the author. Objectively people don't leave their home country and seek to live in a racist oppressive land. Indeed as early as 1814 Governor Macquarie established a school for aboriginal children and one of its students won first prize in the school board examinations. Such provided examples are clearly not consistent with the racism narrative. Dr Sufi's persuasively presented contribution to the debate has filled a void in the popular literature providing a much needed alternative for any enquiring mind. An engaging, scholarly and well-researched contribution which is a must read."

Eric Abetz — Former Leader of the Government in the Senate.

"*I have long believed that we Australians have been the losers from our lack of interest in our history. So often it is either ignored or taught badly - often with intent in pursuit of unhelpful political agendas. This excellent book by Dr Sherry Sufi explains why our history, good and bad, matters greatly. As Churchill had it, a culture which fails to pass on its story, including that of its beliefs and its heroes, is in effect saying that that culture is without value and meaning, thus leaving its young without a sense of place and direction and therefore easily persuaded. Now more than ever we need to rediscover and understand our foundational values, as the raging storms around us threaten to cast us onto the rocks.*"

John Anderson — 11th Deputy Prime Minister of Australia.

"*There couldn't be a more perfect time for this book, as Australians ask themselves who they really are and what role race has or has not played in their extraordinary history. Eschewing the emotional vitriol of the left, Dr Sherry Sufi looks at the Australian story through logic, facts, data and personal experience. This is the book we have all been longing to read.*"

Rowan Dean — Author and Sky News Host.

"*If you are tired of people running down Australia as a racist and broken country, this book is for you. Dr Sherry Sufi meets these accusations with persuasive counter-arguments in clear prose. A must read for those who seek a balanced perspective on the relationship between Australia's past and present.*"

Andrew Hastie — Shadow Defence Minister of Australia.

About the Author

Sherry Sufi is a Western Australian Author, Columnist and Political Commentator.

He holds a Bachelor of Arts (Philosophy), a Diploma of Information Systems, a Master of Arts (Politics and International Studies), a Master of History and a Doctor of Philosophy.

His PhD thesis was on language and nationalism. It's available as a book via Connor Court. He speaks, reads and writes multiple languages.

Since 2015, he has served as Chairman of the WA Liberal Party's Policy Committee. In 2019, he was awarded a Meritorious Service Award for his continued services to the Party.

He was a Senior Fellow at the *Centre for the Australian Way of Life* at the Institute of Public Affairs.

Sherry has been a Contributor for Sky News Australia where he has published articles and made appearances on live television.

He stood as a Liberal Senate Candidate for Western Australia at the 2022 Federal Election.

He was the State Coordinator for Fair Australia's No campaign in WA at the referendum in 2023.

His articles have been published in *The Australian, The West Australian, SkyNews.com.au, The Daily Telegraph, The Spectator, Fairfax Media, The Epoch Times, PerthNow, Times of Israel* and *The Jerusalem Post*.

The views expressed in this book are his own.

W: www.sherrysufi.com
F: www.facebook.com/SherrySufiPhD/
T: https://twitter.com/SherrySufi

Starting Thoughts

I've lost count how many times I've seen folks left wondering after finishing a book if the author's goal was to confuse the heck out of the reader.

It's a fair question. Like, why would you use big words and also take forever to get to the main point.

This book *isn't* like that. It's jargon-free and also aimed at regular folks.

What it brings you is a long awaited defence of Australia against three popular accusations of our times.

One, that it's a racist country. Two, that it was built on 'stolen land'. Three, that it doesn't even have a way of life.

Now, I'm not one to assume that those who believe these accusations to be true are necessarily acting in bad faith.

I believe most are well-intentioned Australians.

I respect them for wanting to level the playing field for those they genuinely believe to be disadvantaged.

Even if we disagree on tactics, neither can we fault their motivations, nor can we disagree with every part of their diagnosis.

We do respectfully disagree on *some* parts and those are addressed in this book.

There's plenty in Australia's past for us to learn from, in its present for us to celebrate and in its future for us to make *even* better.

This book is a modest contribution in our nation's quest to become the best version of ourselves. Enjoy the read.

Table of Contents

1

Introduction: Defining Australia

The lucky country. The land of opportunity. Working Man's Paradise. It has been described as many things — none mutually exclusive. But, what is Australia? Intuitively, we know that it's an English-speaking country with a population of roughly 25 million at the time this book was written. It's situated just south of Far Eastern Asia. It brands itself as a free and democratic country with equality of opportunity for all its citizens, and it is. It has rule of law, a free press, no state religion, no military conscription, universal education and universal healthcare. To the extent that stereotypes might hold true, its people do enjoy the sun, the surf and their barbecues.

Sports are appreciated throughout the year, cricket during the summer and footy during the winter. There is no distinct cuisine in the same sense as what sushi is to Japan, or what spaghetti is to Italy, or what nachos are to Mexico. This lack of culinary distinctness is common across cosmopolitan societies and Australia is no exception. But, meat pies and sausage rolls would probably be the closest thing. Vegemite is a form of spread that's considered uniquely Australian, but it's nowhere near as popular at home as it's often presumed to be abroad.

Australians are considered a laid back people with a 'no nonsense' attitude who usually like to look after our mates. Outside Australia, and to a lesser extent within it, the likes of comedian-actor Paul Hogan and the late crocodile hunter Steve Irwin have come to personify what a typical Australian is.[1] Although that portrayal has been challenged in recent times as Australian society becomes more sensitive to gender and ethnic diversity. Australians love a good yarn. That is, sharing stories and having a chinwag. But usually not on religion and politics. That's pretty much Australia in a nutshell.

This caricature has traditionally worked great for travel brochures and pop culture references in Hollywood. Yet it actually oversimplifies who and what we are to the point that we end up doing a great disservice to our exceptionalism as a country. Besides bringing us lots of curious tourists, that vegemite and croc-hunter version of Australia does well enough to embody the proverbial thousand words a picture finds easy enough to tell. The point of this book is to go beyond the tourism-friendly stereotypes.

Its chapters tell you the untold words otherwise left out of the picture frame about what Australia really is and what it isn't. In comparison to the conflict-prone histories of Europe and the Americas, we in Australia have no real track record of remotely comparable racial or ethnic tensions, religious or sectarian divisions, nor the kind of internal divisions that often lead to civil wars, revolutions and popular assassinations. How good is that? Australia has been lucky enough to be isolated from the rest of the world and to find its own unique path forwards as a society and a nation.

What is it about Australia that continues to attract millions of newcomers from around the world to come and settle here, chase their dreams, get an education and a job, earn a decent living, start a family, buy a house, raise children and retire in peace? There is a defining belief across the country that in this place, with a bit of hard work, just about anyone can ensure that tomorrow is better than yesterday. Those who seek a future that brings more comfort, security and prosperity than the past can, and do get there in the end. In this place, millions of Australians continue to fulfil their aspirations for a happy, successful and meaningful life.

As for those who, for whatever reason, find life more challenging than the rest, guess what? In this place, we have countless safety nets to minimise their hardships and bring them on the journey with the rest. All of this gives us some idea why not many Australians prefer migrating overseas from Australia[2] and so many from overseas do prefer migrating to Australia.[3] Remember that a satisfied population doesn't usually have much incentive to leave its homeland, unless it's for a holiday. There are good reasons why Australia is, on balance, the great country that it is, and this book brings these good reasons to you in plain lingo. But hang on, before we get stuck into all that, let's have a quick think about why Australia needs to be defined beyond its stereotypes in the first place. As in, what is the point of this book? Well, let's see.

In an ideal world, such an exercise wouldn't be needed. Everyone would be on the same page about the goodness of Australia and we'd all march forwards as one and free, as our national anthem proclaims. We'd all share the great opportunities afforded to those lucky few that have the privilege of calling this place home. In such a world, there would be consensus that Australia, like any sovereign country, has the right to preserve itself in its ideal form. The reality is, we don't have these luxuries. Australia presently sits on a trajectory that is steering it towards the eventual erosion of its institutions, traditions, values and way of life.

Not only does this grim reality make it necessary to define who and what we are supposed to be, it even makes it an obligation to discuss whether each of us could do our bit to celebrate and enrich the Australian way of life, instead of letting it be substituted with something else. That's the challenge this book tackles head on. To be clear from the get go, neither is this a history textbook, nor should it be read like one. This is a case for Australia. We can't define Australia nor its essence without addressing some of the defining political and cultural challenges the country faces at present. In particular, those challenges that have largely gone unaddressed. In doing so, we will refer to the past as and when needed. The take home message is that Australia is great for reasons that go beyond the commercial stereotype. It is great because its way of life, although slowly deteriorating, is still great. Its way of life is great because those who settled here with the aspiration to make a future for themselves were great. This is the untold story this book seeks to tell.

Remember that nations are founded upon stories. Be it America's founding legend as a shining City Upon a Hill, so culturally alike and yet so unlike continental Europe at the same time. Be it Israel's origins with

Moses leading the Hebrews across the Red Sea, Joshua leading them into the promised land and King David establishing the first Kingdom. Be it Romulus and Remus and the founding of Rome, often co-opted by present-day Italian nationalists.

In the grand scheme of things, it hardly matters whether these stories are wholly true, partly true, or altogether made up. What's fascinating is not only that such stories exist across all cultures, but more importantly, virtually all cultures prioritise their preservation and transmission from one generation to the next with relentless consistency. This tendency embodies that very primordial human need to belong to something that goes beyond us, the mere individual. Just as bees connect to a hive, ants build colonies and birds fly together in murmurations, humans too have a deep yearning to belong to and commune with others who share something in common with us.

It isn't enough to say that stories are simply pivotal to this process of continuity, stories are in fact the starting point of our own murmuration. When let's say Anthony Albanese is sworn in as Prime Minister, that may be the start of a new government, but it isn't the start of a new story. It is, in fact, the continuation of something that cuts across time and space. And that makes him the 31st episode of a story that began in 1901, with Edmund Barton as its first chapter – the proverbial pilot episode. Stories shape communities all over the world. Some are defined as religious or sectarian, as cultural or ethnic, as ideological or something else.

Does Australia have a story? If so, is it one we can all be proud of? Yes, it does to the first part. Ours is nothing as theatrical as Romulus nor Moses, but we do have a story. Yet the untold part of our story is that of one group of poverty stricken convicts, later free settlers, devoid of education and basic amenities in an age when social status and class defined one's worth as an individual get sent to one of the harshest terrains on earth and their descendants end up turning their godforsaken continent from an open air prison into an industrial paradise in less than a century.

This was either a fluke or a miracle. While there has been an element of serendipity, I for one don't believe it to be a fluke overall. It's when we start understanding how we became what we have in the improbable timeframe in which we did it, we will have found the answer to the second part. For me, that's a big yes. Ours is a story we can all be proud of. The reason for this isn't because our story is a perfect one. No country's story is perfect, ours included. We can all be proud of our story because it has a place for everyone. As with many stories, once they've been told by multiple voices at multiple times, it often becomes difficult to isolate the authentic voice from one fraught with Chinese whispers. Australia's story is a bit like that.

Those that have told its story in recent decades have too often told it with such whispers that make Australia out to be a 'racist' nation built on 'stolen land' that supposedly lacks a distinct enough way of life. Nations are made up of individuals and it goes without saying, individuals come with diverse attitudes. The vast majority couldn't care less about race, but there are always some who hold prejudicial views. Some individuals can have racist attitudes in almost any nation imaginable. But to say that the nation itself is institutionally or systematically racist is far too great a stretch. Not only is it invalid but also a dangerous claim which gives the world, as well as future generations of our own citizens, a reputation that modern Australia doesn't deserve.

Humans have always wandered the earth from one place to another in search of a better life. Some got to a particular piece of soil earlier than others. Lands have always been settled and resettled. There is no such thing as 'Ceylon' and 'Rhodesia' on the world map anymore. But there are 'Sri Lanka' and 'Zimbabwe'. Lands can change hands. They can change names. But they're not exactly stolen, unless we're talking about a piece of private property within a sovereign jurisdiction. Australia was discovered, settled and deemed to have been conquered over time in accordance with international conventions and norms as applicable in the late 1700s.

That's not where the whispers stop either. It has too often been suggested that Australia doesn't even have a culture or way of life worth celebrating, let alone preserving for future generations. Those who subscribe to these accusations, usually do so with absolute certainty. They then proceed to argue that since Australia doesn't have a culture or way of life, what's there to preserve? Their main prescription is to allow for the gradual penetration of the Australian way of life with alternative values in the name of promoting diversity and harmony. But not only does Australia have a unique way of life, that way of life is what's responsible for making it the lucky country, the land of opportunity and the working man's paradise.

Many of those who disagree with these whispers about our past too often lack any hope that Australia can even survive as the nation we've so far known. This book brings hope. Despite being a truly exceptional country, Australia has arrived at this difficult junction mainly due to the cultural amnesia that is prevalent in the imaginations of far too great a number of Australians. We are so focussed on living in the moment that we have completely abandoned any sense of connection with the past. When the public doesn't care to learn its own nation's story and to pass it down to future generations, the deficit left behind gets replenished with the whispers of self-doubt that skew public opinion towards the beliefs that we're a racist country built on stolen land without a way of life.

At the core of this cultural amnesia lies a widespread lack of appreciation for the discipline of history. This part isn't typical of all nations. It would be far too great an oversimplification to allege that the general public in all countries finds its own nation's story boring and irrelevant. The fact that we in Australia do, is quite unique. We're unfortunately in the minority of nations where the past isn't cared for with much excitement. It is precisely due to the fact that our cultural amnesia is the main factor responsible for creating the requisite conditions that resulted in the emergence of self-doubt that the starting chapter of this book will deal with Australia's relationship with its past and present. By the time you're done reading this book, I hope you will be ready to join me in this quest to maintain a balanced perspective on Australia, to feel confident about making sense of some of the crucial debates happening in our own time that require informed decisions.

2

The Past and the Present:

Cultural Amnesia

No country on the world map has been around forever. There are older ones and newer ones. But each has a starting point. Each also has a story to go with it. These stories are often complex. They involve multiple actors with competing interests. There is hardly a country that doesn't have a complex relationship with its past. Human beings are a nomadic species who constantly wander the earth in search of a better life. Long before the birth of spoken language, agriculture, written laws and pottery in ancient Sumer around 3200 BCE, the hunter-gatherers were constantly migrating from one place to another either based on variations in the weather or the availability of resources, or the relative prospects of a risk to their survival. Due to thousands of years of humans moving around, there is literally no place left on earth that has only ever been exclusively settled by a single group of people. Australia is no different in this respect.

The land on which Australia sits was inhabited by people who have come to be known as Indigenous Australians for what some estimate to be 60,000 years. Europeans began to settle this place from 1788 onwards. This, at times cordial, and at times tense, exchange between the two is the foundation of Australia's story. Like all national stories, this too is a complex one. Plenty of books have been written on the subject. Different historians have offered different points of view on the nature and circumstances of this relationship. There are at least two identifiable schools of thought among Australian historians. There is the view that the interaction between the two was mostly benign and clashes were the exception, rather than the rule. This school of thought is colloquially referred to as the 'whitewash' camp, although nobody in this camp refers to one's self in those terms.

The other view is that the interaction was mostly quite hostile and clashes were all too frequent.[4] This school of thought is colloquially referred to as the 'black armband' camp, although again, nobody in the camp actually refers to one's self that way either. The so-called 'whitewash' version of Australia's story was, once upon a time, the norm. In recent decades, the so-called black armband version has gained more currency across Australian university campuses and the media. The concept of 'truth' creates an uncomfortable feeling in the mind of the historian. This is because a good historian always seeks it and yet the more we learn about a particular topic, the more we end up realising that usually there isn't a single version of truth. That's right, truth can mean different things to different characters in the same story. As the stories of countries correspond with the core of one's group identity, the way we feel about our nation's past naturally ends up becoming an emotional matter. It is difficult to strike the right balance and maintain an impartial perspective. Without a doubt, Australia has faced some serious challenges in recent decades as conservatives fear that one account of its settlement has come to outgrow the other in terms of its popularity.

Everything discussed here might sound straightforward enough to follow so far. The challenging part is to work out which school of thought we should subscribe to. It is a serious matter with serious consequences. How we feel about the past ultimately impacts the political decisions we make on a day-to-day basis. It isn't always obvious for something as basic as this to be realised. The past is perceived as remote by the modern observer and remoteness is always relative. Australia only goes back under two and a half centuries. That's more than twice the expectancy of the human lifespan in developing countries, but in the grand scheme of things, it is very recent. England traces its origins back to 1066 and the Battle of Hastings. Arguable at best, but that's more or less the official version of England's starting point. Australia barely goes back to 1788.

There's no shortage of books on Australian history. Except, written by academics, for academics, not really for regular folks. The intention of this book is not to add to the weight of such books in the collection of Australian literature. Rather than discussing the past itself, this book as a whole and this chapter in particular explores our relationship with the past. It helps us realise that our longstanding apathy towards the discipline of history has ultimately helped create the requisite conditions to enable some to impose on us a revisionist account of the past that makes many present-day Australians feel a sense of collective guilt. We can't confront these challenges of the day, let alone be able to address them, unless we are able to truly appreciate the nature of how the past works and how those who record it see it. It is only when we are given a persuasive account of what history even deals with, what historians do, and why it should matter to us, that we will be able to consider ourselves as a nation ready to move forwards with confidence in who we are as a collection of aspiring individuals.

The present is a continuation of the past. Yet not many Australians would necessarily list history as our favourite subject in high school. Many would openly admit to having little time for thinking about the past, even for the sake of social conversations. As a nation, we're programmed to live in the present. This cuts across both directions in time. Many often don't care enough for the long-term future either. Many would struggle to tell you where we might be in 20 years from now. This tendency to want to focus on the now is built into our cultural psyche, and no doubt, has its pros and cons. It often does help us get over stuff fast and move on. Yet at the same time, it limits both our curiosity for where we came from and concern for where we might be headed. That, in turn, limits our ability to make informed decisions about our society in the present, which is ultimately shaped by events that happened in the past.

The less familiar we are with the past, the greater our disconnect from the present. A large part of this disregard for history comes down to a misperception about what the field actually involves. Too often, we tend to take history as a collection of 'fun facts' and a historian is widely perceived to be someone who memorises those fun facts. I've lost count the number of times I've been asked by mates to join their table for a quiz night. Since I studied history, the presumption is that by having me there, our table would end up winning. On some occasions, this does work. On other occasions, it doesn't. Being a historian doesn't automatically mean one's brain has all the answers to those trivia questions.

To give an example, a quiz night question might ask 'Name the fourth Prime Minister of Australia?' and you may not know who that was because, we as Australians even struggle to name our first Prime Minister, let alone the fourth. Back in 1999, there was a full-on campaign to make citizens aware who Sir Edmund Barton our first Prime Minister was in the lead up to the centenary of Federation.[5] Similarly in 2011, Cricket Australia surveyed a number of Australian international test cricketers at the time about the same question and most didn't know who the first Prime Minister was either. The video clip of this is available on YouTube.[6]

It's probably fair to say that Australians are still more likely to guess the name of the first PM than the fourth. It was George Reid, by the way. Testing participants on this level of basic and not entirely useful info is what quiz nights are all about. A casual nerd that spends all day memorising fun facts might be who you want on your quiz table, but the professional historian is far from fit for that purpose.

The historian would look at the social and political circumstances prevalent in the lead up to Federation (1901). This would involve looking at debates over the pros and cons of Federation that took place between that early generation of Australia's founding pioneers, one of whom happens to be Edmund Barton and another, George Reid. A good historian should be able to tell you what Reid's role, contribution and significance was in the timeframe in which he served as a politician, but it isn't entirely necessary that the chronology alone would be the main focus.

The analyses around historical events and figures, who they were, what they said, what they did, or why what they did matters at all are far more important than memorising details like dates of birth, or towns of birth, or ordinal ranks that may feature in those quiz night questions. Unless, of course, a significant part of the historian's analysis itself depended on such biographical details, which is rarely the case. I emphasise this point in this chapter before we dive into more fundamental issues because our ability to address them depends on how we think about the past. This point needs to be made because it's rarely made in a manner accessible to the general public. It is common to see history as a collection of uncontested facts, as opposed to a mixture of some elusive facts and many equally if not even more elusive interpretations.

There are plenty of history books which discuss significant figures and analyse events in a particular timeframe. But there aren't nearly enough in the public domain that discuss what people *think* history is, as opposed to what history *actually* is and *why* it should matter to us all. It would be unreasonable to expect Australians to start appreciating history until we first make it clear what its intended purpose even is. In the simplest of terms, the study of history is an analytical investigation into the complex relationships between past events and present realities. The sort of individuals who enter into the profession are those that are naturally curious about understanding how and why the world we live in is shaped the way it is. It is that quest to wrap our heads around the present that leaves us with no choice but to end up developing an insatiable appetite for having a sneak peek into the past. Memorising a list of names, dates and rough descriptions of things like wars fought, or popular sayings by Kings and Generals really shouldn't be and usually aren't the main priority for a disciplined historian.

A historian usually picks a specific time period, or a specific idea or trend, forms a specific research question, and then tries to find answers based on whatever record is available. For instance, one might ask "Why did the United States drop two nuclear bombs on Japan during World War II?". This, of course, was a political decision made by a particular American President in August 1945, but since I wasn't around back then, I couldn't be part of the news cycle of the day. Those that were, would at least be aware of how that decision came about. They would have some level of familiarity with the political complexities and debates in the lead up to that decision as read in the newspapers, heard on the radio and seen on television in weeks and days prior, the same way that most of us who follow the news have some basic familiarity with the key events that are happening in our own time. Although that's not to imply that every one of us is necessarily an expert on events taking place in our time. All that's implied here is that we have this sense of basic familiarity with the things that happen in our own time. No wonder most of us can recall the debates around the marriage vote in 2017 and the Voice vote in 2023. Even if we weren't experts on the subjects being put to us, it is fair to say that members of the general public do have a rough idea of what the two sides of the coin represent in these present-day debates taking place in our own timeframes. When evaluating the distant past, we don't have this luxury.

The eye-witnesses who decide to put pen to paper and start documenting details of events as they happen don't just record plain 'facts' alone. They in fact present their own analyses of how and why they thought things happened the way they did. To consider a relatively recent case for most adults, take the example of the attacks on the World Trade Centre in New York on 11th September 2001. This is a significant event that virtually every adult today would remember vividly enough. While this basic and widespread familiarity doesn't make everyone an expert on the clash between the United States and Al-Qaeda,[7] a small number of those adults would have gone on to present their analyses of the subject. These range from historians, to political scientists, to anthropologists, to sociologists, to criminologists, to journalists, to politicians, to the girl next door who just happens to have an opinion. If these are produced in close proximity to the event in consideration, then they would all be considered primary sources. The further out in the future the observer happens to be from the original event being described, the higher the likelihood of them being considered a secondary source. All else aside, the quality of one's analysis is a separate matter altogether.

In an attempt to find answers to those curious questions, what the historian who wasn't around back then is left with is no choice but to survey both the primary and secondary records that deal with the subject. As outlined using the 9/11 example, the primary record is the material that existed *at the time* of the event or shortly thereafter. In the case of understanding why the United States would drop nukes on Japan during World War II, this might involve our engagement with newspaper clippings, speeches made by President Truman who announced that decision, radio interviews, and black and white television clips, among other things such as White House correspondence documents, declassified minutes to confidential security briefings, and the like. To recap, eye-witness accounts and their analyses do constitute primary sources, while secondary source records concern the analyses presented by others who tend to draw their conclusions based on their analyses of primary source records.

The importance of history as cultural memory for a nation, how to differentiate between primary and secondary sources, and interpreting present-day realities through historical lens are things that might be obvious to trained academics in the humanities and related fields, but they are almost certainly not so commonly known by regular folks. Yet it isn't just professional historians who live in societies that have a history, everyone does. Everyone that belongs to a nation, or an imagined community[8] as it has been called, has a past. The perceived and actual achievements of a nation's past go on to become a great sense of pride with members of the nation that had nothing personal to do with it. So many Americans, for instance, still proudly boast that 'they' have been to the moon and back when referring to Neil Armstrong's Apollo 11 mission that landed on the moon on 20th July 1969 along with Buzz Aldrin.[9]

It works the same way for sports. When an athlete from one's country wins gold at the Olympics, that's not just a victory for her or him, it becomes a victory for the entire nation, essentially whoever happens to be part of that imagined community. Likewise, the perceived and actual misdeeds of a nation's past go on to become a great sense of shame with members of the nation that had nothing personal to do with it. The topic of US President Truman dropping nuclear bombs on Japanese cities of Hiroshima and Nagasaki in August 1945 continues to remain a source of tremendous angst among present-day Americans. Some justify the decision to nuke publicly on the basis that it was to halt Japanese advances and save lives. Others see it as morally abhorrent given it was widely known to the decision makers that those two towns targeted were inhabited by thousands of civilians. The release of Hollywood blockbuster *Oppenheimer* (2023) has in fact reignited this exact debate about the moral implications of nuclear warfare.[10] The closer we look at the past, the more historic baggage we become aware of. Modern Westerners, particularly those of a conservative leaning, would have no trouble taking the credit for their European ancestors producing a document like Magna Carta in 1215, or for the period known as the Enlightenment when Europe is believed to have had its cultural awakening, the Industrial Revolution that gave us countless new technologies and many other similar processes, movements and periods that arguably had a net positive impact on human advancement.

At the same time, the fact that so much of the story of Western civilisation is fraught with slavery and military encounters with militarily weaker native populations in conquered lands also continues to be a source of anxiety. The left of politics in Western countries tends to mainly focus on the bad that came about as a result of European imperialism. The right of politics in Western countries tends to mainly focus on the good that came out of European imperialism. Sometimes the differences in narration and interpretation end up being so vast that instead of appearing like two chapters of the same story, their accounts start to seem more like two separate stories altogether. This is the challenge that modern Australia faces: we have an educated class that is torn within itself. Those on the left accuse those on the right of being heartless and turning a blind eye to past injustices inflicted upon native populations. Those on the right accuse those on the left of exaggerating the bad bits of Western history and downplaying its positive achievements.

Meanwhile, the regular Australian out in the suburban heartland remains typically indifferent to any interest in, nor care for the past. This indifference is far from ideal because when we have two educated minorities competing over how we should make sense of our nation's past, the louder and more persistent of the two can often end up having more impact with the general public. Not always due to the merits of the argument, but due to the loudness of its voice. It just happens to be the case that in present time, many conservatives believe that voices of the left have become louder and as such, more influential than the voices of the right. Aspects of this perception may be debatable in their own right and conservatives may not be as persecuted as they often believe themselves to be considering they do have their own publications and broadcast units too, but, there is validity in the basic claim that opinions of the left are generally more common within academic circles. This is a challenge that remains widespread across the Anglosphere. It has been well-realised by famous thinkers from across different disciplines in the likes of Steven Pinker and Jonathan Haidt who have over the years played an active role in the non-profit organisation the Heterodox Academy which aims to achieve more viewpoint diversity in academic practice.

To return to the main point, we have a population with widespread cultural amnesia that results from our complete lack of interest in understanding, let alone appreciating, our own history. We think of history as just a compendium of fun facts that have no use outside of quiz nights. We have top tier athletes representing our nation who struggle to name who the first Prime Minister that led the nation they are representing was. Meanwhile, that small minority of activists from both the left and the right have, for decades, been talking among themselves about how to interpret the past. Now, we have a situation where the louder and more widespread voice is beginning to fill the void of public apathy. Many conservatives believe this isn't happening because it's right, but because it's loud. As public opinion on social issues in Australian society tends to shift more towards the left, this can change the direction of public policy debates and voting patterns. A population that either doesn't know its own history or only knows a version of it that lacks nuance is a population that opens itself up to manipulation by the political class, from both within and outside. The antidote to all this is an informed population that appreciates the complexities and maturely subscribes to a balanced viewpoint.

There is little value in subscribing to either the so-called 'black armband' view or the 'whitewash' view of the past. It is neither productive to presume most Australian history is something to be ashamed of, nor is it productive to presume that most Australian history gives us nothing to regret. Balance is the key. That's where wisdom lies and this book is a modest attempt to bring that to the reader in accessible language, free from academic jargon.

While this is not intended to be a history book, one of its goals is to encourage young Australians to start taking an active interest in history and politics. There are countless benefits to this. Informed citizens may not always get it right, but we would have a far higher chance of making sensible decisions than the alternative option of letting our unfamiliarity be taken advantage of by a small number of activists. Now that we have discussed what the lay of the land is, it's time to confront the challenges ahead as informed citizens.

Australia stands accused. There are those who say, Australia is a racist country. I acknowledge why some see it that way, but I don't entirely agree. There are those who say, Australia was built on stolen land, I see where they might be coming from, but I don't entirely agree. There are those who say, Australia doesn't even have a way of life, and again, I understand what leads some to come to that conclusion, but I don't believe it's entirely valid. Just as it is a very Australian thing to welcome the right of our critics to say things we don't fully agree with, the same right applies to us. We too are free to say our bit to respond to our critics as long as we're operating within bounds of mutual respect and presenting our arguments in good faith. That's pretty much what the rest of this book tries to do.

What follows in coming chapters are discussions that need to be had, but are either rarely had, or usually only had inside echo chambers preaching to the converted. Sure, I agree it's often comforting for the mind to surround ourselves with those who see the world the same way as us, after all that's why 'like-mindedness' continues to be a defining feature of friendships and relationships. But too much hanging around with those who more or less think identically to ourselves on the big issues breeds one-sided beliefs. It shuts us out from having our views challenged and tested for consistency. It also sows the foundations for social rifts which turn into political rifts. The fix is not to think the same, but to engage in dialogue. For all we know, we may be the ones wrong and others may teach us something worth learning. If not, the other way around.

3

Is Australia a racist country?

No social concept irritates Australians more than racism. This is for two distinct yet seemingly contradictory reasons. The first is that we are naturally committed to justice and a fair go as part of our way of life and racism goes against all that. It tries to highlight barriers between individuals based on ancestral differences. That makes us feel uncomfortable. Whenever Australians hear reports of a racist incident at a workplace, on a sporting field, a schoolyard or anywhere else, the general response is to be frustrated by it. Some even end up sympathising with the perceived or actual victim without hearing the full story. This is how deeply ingrained our cultural predisposition to fairness and equality really is.

The second reason why racism annoys us may seem at odds with the first, but it actually isn't. It's that many Australians suspect that claims of racism are often misreported or worse yet, deliberately exploited for ulterior motives. An example would be a batsman being given out LBW in a game of cricket and claiming that the umpire was racist. Or a university student receiving a poor mark for an assignment and claiming the Professor was racist. Or an employee being made redundant and claiming the employer was racist. Instead of focussing on ways to lift up one's sporting or academic or professional game, externalising the blame for our struggles on supposedly racist umpires, professors and prospective employers does tend to concern many Australians.

Looking at reasons one and two together also highlights the point that Australians generally do know how to differentiate between legitimate and imaginary forms of racism. This reinforces my longstanding point that Australians tend to be naturally sceptical and often have the ability to tell when something isn't fair dinkum. While it's safe to say that many Australians have this intuitive sense about what racism is, if most were asked to define it in a single sentence the way we get taught to let's say define a 'noun' back in primary school, more than a few would end up struggling. This is due to the overall lack of critical thought put into racism as a concept, what it is, why it exists, how long it's been around in society and the like.

Exceptions aside, if things get too deep, Australians generally start to tune out. This can be both a good and a bad thing. It's a good thing because it shows that we're a nation of lighthearted folks who keep our social convos fun and simple. Nothing wrong with that. At the same time, it can be bad because if we're dealing with an abstract concept that continues to dominate far too great a chunk of everyday media commentary and we as citizens are required to take a stance on key public policy positions, then that indifference most certainly would work to our disadvantage.

Due to this lack of critical thought on the topic of racism, many Australians remain susceptible to being guilt-tripped about racism in situations where none exists. Australians may recognise that racism exists, but dislike being told *they* are racist. There is nothing surprising about this. Remember that most people also recognise that selfishness and greed might exist, but that doesn't mean they appreciate being told they're selfish or greedy themselves. In an ideal world, we wouldn't need to include a topic such as racism in a book like this. Neither do we live in an ideal world, nor do I believe that ignoring a topic as repeatedly discussed as racism is an option for us.

In recent decades, we have been reminded time and time again, that Australia was born out of racism towards the Indigenous people and that it continues to remain a racist country to date. These reminders come from some of the most influential sections of our society. Regular Australians aren't trained historians. It'd be unreasonable to expect that they should have the interest, time and resources to survey the past and make their own judgements on such contentious topics.

If the idea that Australia has a big racism problem is repeated with great persistence, as it often has been in recent decades then chances are, such a thought would start to penetrate sizeable chunks of public opinion. The country's academics are usually the ones who decide what sort of narratives get taught to students on university campuses. Journalists hold similar power over those who read newspapers. News anchors can influence millions of people at once using the power of television broadcast.

The over-supply of public and political commentary on racism is seen differently by the two sides of politics. Exceptions aside, those on the progressive-left generally argue that we've had issues in the past with racism and still have a long way to go in fully overcoming it, so the constant reminders are justified. Those on the conservative-right generally argue there is an over-supply of views because our so-called academic elites and the mainstream media like to exaggerate the past and guilt trip the current generation for the perceived and actual racism of earlier generations, so the constant reminders are not justified.

Despite the fact that Australia remains one of the most inclusive and pluralistic societies in the world, like most English-speaking Western countries, it too has managed to force itself into a suffocating corner on the issue of racism. Recovery from this position looks challenging. Racism has been made out to be a far more amplified and insidious social concept than it actually is in Australia's case. As we share a language and pop culture with the United States, often their far more intense and regular experiences with racial tensions are broadcast in the Australian press. Themes depicting racism are also portrayed in famous Hollywood films such as *To Kill a Mockingbird* (1962), *Mississippi Burning* (1988) and *12 Years a Slave* (2013) among hundreds more.[11] They inevitably end up impacting the way Australians feel about the severity of racial problems and the urgency to fix them. This case of a foreign problem attracting domestic conversations at home results in immense pressure on the political class to borrow American ideas, terminologies and in more recent times Twitter hashtags to import those struggles here.

It must be acknowledged that Australia has a complex relationship with its past. There is hardly a country in the world that doesn't. In most cases, governments control the way the citizens engage with the past. Since Australia happens to be a democracy that is generally committed to freedom of thought, speech and press, this means that our perceived and actual sins can't be left hidden inside the closet for too long. Some academic or journalist will inevitably end up digging through the archives and making it a goal to expose the perceived and actual mistreatment of Indigenous Australians and various other groups by British settlers on this land.

That said, Australia's experiences are in no way comparable to those of the United States where the past was marred with constant struggles between European settlers and the natives, centuries of slave trade and ownership, the struggles against slavery, abolition, the Ku Klux Klan and the Civil Rights movement. These are all chapters of American history, not ours. We have nothing of the sort. Yet news reports of supposed and actual racial tensions in the United States on Australian prime time television and on front pages of Australian newspapers become the lens through which we start filtering our own experiences. Because we share a language and culture with the Americans, their issues being broadcast on our media start shaping the way we feel about certain topics at home.

Somewhere in the process, Indigenous Australians have been made out to be the equivalent of African Americans, and Anglo-Celtic Australians are made out to be what critics perceive as oppressive white colonisers. A prime example of this was the aftermath of George Lloyd's tragic murder in May 2020.[12] The hashtag *Black Lives Matter* movement essentially reached Australian shores and was given a disproportionate amount of news coverage. This further reinforces the need for us to get right back to basics and engage with the topic of racism with a level of critical thought we otherwise see missing from public discussions on the topic. The rest of this chapter presents us with an opportunity to delve into this.

The single biggest reason why most debates on racism get nowhere in Australia, and elsewhere in the Anglosphere, is due to the inability to reach consensus on how to define it. Unless two or more participants in a discussion had the same concept of racism, they would be talking at cross purposes and that isn't constructive. A definition for a concept in a critical discussion serves the same purpose as a piece of legislation during a trial. Lawyers on opposite sides of a case might have clashing opinions about whether or not legislation has been breached, they don't usually clash on what the legislation is. Lawyers on opposite sides are only able to assess whether or not there has been a breach of that legislation and offer their reasoning to support their competing viewpoints. They're able to do this because they're familiar with the same piece of legislation in the first place.

Debating racism, or any abstract concept for that matter, without a consensus-based definition is the equivalent of two lawyers arguing over a case without looking at the same legislation. Australia's lack of a standard definition for racism has its reasons. In authoritarian or single party countries, the government has the luxury to define a certain social concept and enforce a single standardised definition on its citizens through its state-controlled media and its state-sanctioned education curriculum. Open and democratic countries like Australia and those of the Anglosphere don't have this luxury to the same scale. Our embrace of different opinions and beliefs often works to our own detriment but we remain committed to upholding our ideals regardless.

The political pendulum in Australia's two-party system ensures that the government changes from left-to-right or right-to-left every two to three terms. The two sides have competing perspectives on how to engage with the past. This is the first challenge when it comes to enforcing a single definition. Even if one government enforced its version of events by altering the curriculum, the next government would simply change it back to where it thinks the balance should be set on how the past is perceived. For unconventional countries, enforcing a single version of events framed in a specific manner aimed at boosting patriotic sentiments is much easier.

It is countries of the Anglosphere including Australia that happen to be the exception. Due to our commitment to doing the right thing by our values, with or without realising, we end up giving up certain luxuries available at the disposal of other societies. For the exact same reason, no official government has yet been able to enforce its concept of what racism is. This is not to say that racism is impossible to define. Nor is it to say that attempts haven't been made through legislation. In fact, we have strict discriminatory laws in Australia. The point is, at the cultural level, it is difficult to define it. There is a sense of synchronicity between law and culture in other societies that we seem to lack. The bottom line is, once we have this definition, we can use it to make certain assessments about Australian society to advance that discussion about our own supposed and actual relationship with racial difference.

Racism can either mean a superiority complex (belief) about one's own race over others. Or it can mean discrimination (practice) against members of another race *due to* race. If a black person chooses not to employ a white person, that's not automatic racism. If a black person chooses not to employ a white person *because* they're white, that's racism. As we can already see from this basic reflection, racism is both a belief (a subset of supremacism) and a practice (a subset of discrimination). Any discussion on racism has to deal with racism in both these senses.

Since racism is a subset of supremacism, it only makes sense that we also define this parent idea. Supremacism is the idea that one's own community group is superior to the rest based on whatever tier of identity one feels more strongly connected to. Note that human identity is a multi-tiered concept. The same individual can be a *New Yorker* by region, an *American* by nationality, a *Catholic* by sect, a *Christian* by religion, an *Anglophone* by language, an *Anglo-Celt* by ethnicity, a *Westerner* by civilisation and *white* by race at the same time.

Each of these subsets of one's identity could be weaponised into a form of raging nationalism. Often, as to which tier of one's identity takes precedence for an individual over the others comes down to one's upbringing, education and personal circumstances. Some feel greater loyalty and pride in one's religion over ethnicity, others feel greater commitment to their ethnicity over religion. Each tier carries the potential to boost an individual's sense of pride to the point that one starts bordering on the edges of supremacism. Since supremacist thoughts can be grounded in any one of these various tiers of one's identity, that makes nationalism, ethnocentrism, civilisationism, religious fundamentalism, sectarianism and racism all subsets of supremacism.

It's impossible to be a Christian without having an opinion why being

Christian is superior to being Buddhist. Likewise, it's impossible to be a Catholic without having an opinion why being a Catholic is superior to being a Protestant. It's impossible to be a proud American without having some rationale about what makes America greater than other countries. It is precisely this predisposition towards American exceptionalism that Donald Trump's campaign slogan in 2016 was 'Make America Great Again'.[13] In fact, if we look closely at the lyrics of virtually any country's national anthem, we find just about all of them are fraught with varying degrees of pride with supremacist tendencies. It's impossible to be a proud Westerner without having some beliefs about the superiority and universality of what are perceived as Western values: democracy, individualism, freedom and human rights regardless of whether you are on the progressive-left or the conservative-right.

While each identity tier may have the potential to form the basis for supremacist thoughts, they don't all attract the same rebuke. A t-shirt with a 'Proud to be a New Yorker' or a 'Proud to be an American' on it might be acceptable, but one that says 'Proud to be white' could land you in hot water in seconds of being publicly spotted. This is not because we don't recognise race as a thing, we do. It's because race is considered a 'no go' zone. It's just not a topic anyone wants to discuss, except where strictly necessary. For instance, if the same person who can't wear that t-shirt went missing or ran away from a crime scene, the first bit of detail the police would release to the public to help identify them would in fact be their race. There is a kind of irony in that. According to present-day norms, it is acceptable to be described as white by someone else, but not to express any pride in that identity subset.

These standards may be arbitrary but they're not enforced with consistency across all cases. An African American still has a far higher likelihood of getting away with wearing a t-shirt that says 'Proud to be black'. Far from being seen as inherently racist, that might even be seen by some as empowering. This is because not all colours are equal when it comes to politics and power. The general assumption on the part of critics is that whites are the ruling class and represent power, while blacks are the marginalised minority and represent oppression. In the minds of those who see it this way, open expression of pride in whiteness is inherently racist but in blackness is not. This may seem like double-standards to conservatives, but if we put ourselves in the shoes of minorities we can see why many members of these groups and their progressive supporters see things this way.

Race is considered to be the most contentious of all tiers of human identity. This is despite the fact that throughout history, there have been far more instances of supremacist havoc caused in the name of religious fundamentalism, sectarianism, ethnocentrism and nationalism. Yet these forms of supremacism have not only survived to date, they even continue to be widely tolerated throughout the world despite being more destructive overall.

Humanity has proven itself capable of war with mass casualties in the name of literally every one of these subsets of supremacism. Yet the subset that continues to drive tremendous anxiety and ends up attracting endless public commentary and policy focus as a priority is the one that is closest to extinction in our time, and that's racism. To understand why racism continues to bother humans in general and Australians to the scale that it does while other far more destructive tiers of identity are subconsciously considered more acceptable, it's imperative to take a close look at humanity's first contact with concepts of race and the chain of events that helped shape these attitudes.

For most of world history, people didn't see each other as members of this race, or that race. Although ethnicity is not a new concept.[14] Race is an elusive and relatively recent concept to define. Before the Industrial Revolution in the late 1700s, most people were peasants and farmers who neither had the need to travel outside their own villages, nor did they have the means to travel long distances. Their only exposure to other humans meant those more or less identical to themselves, except foreign invaders or neighbouring nations and tribes with whom their leaders had clashed.

The English and the French might both be racially the same but they clashed with each other on the battlefield for some 800 years from the Battle of Hastings in 1066 to the Battle of Waterloo in 1815.[15] Supremacism was around back then, throughout history, the belief that 'my people are superior to yours' but it wasn't based on race since people didn't consciously know what race was the way we think of it today. Those other tiers of human identity for the most part served as the basis behind most ancient to classical to medieval to early modern ideas of supremacism, until the concept of race entered the mix.

Race didn't appear overnight. It developed over a gradual period of time after Christopher Columbus landed in the Americas in 1492 and European voyagers began coming in close contact with non-Europeans who appeared significantly different from themselves. They instantly had to come to terms with why others were so different in appearance and why those other 'races' in newly discovered lands seemed to have less developed technologies and customs that seemed 'barbaric' to the eyes of Europeans.

In trying to come up with explanations to account for these visible differences, it's not surprising that a class of thinkers emerged that took it upon itself to find the answers. They have been described as 'Orientalists' for their curious interest in studying the Orient which initially meant any non-European lands and their various cultures. Later, the Orient came to be understood as a narrower reference to the regions of North Africa, the Middle East, the Subcontinent and other parts of Asia. Palestinian American literary critic Edward Said is best known for his book *Orientalism* (1978) which tries to look critically at Western representations of the East. He argued that the West's understanding of the East or 'The Orient' was not based on truth, but on a constructed image aimed at reinforcing Western dominance over these lands and subjugating their peoples.[16]

The idea that Europeans were 'racially' superior to the rest became the most natural and convenient explanation to account for all things in a single place. From why other races seemed unattractive to them, to why other cultures had supposedly 'barbaric' customs, to why other societies had less advanced technology, racial hierarchy became the one-size-fits-all theory that explained everything. As people up until that time had already been accustomed to other forms of supremacist ideas, it wasn't at all difficult nor surprising for race to join the club and take over as the basis for continued beliefs in the superiority of one's group over another.

Just as ideas of religious supremacy were legitimised in earlier centuries through divine mandates, ideas of racial supremacy were legitimised through a scientific mandate which, by the mid-1800s, had gained ascendancy over religion across the Western world. These renewed forms of race-based supremacism (or what we simply call 'racism') were in many ways even more concerning because they appealed to reason, instead of blind faith. They were supposedly accompanied by evidence that seemed both empirical and irrefutable in the eyes of observers at the time.

It isn't surprising that as those ideas began to emerge and be debated among the European elite, they would go on to form the basis for continued justification for discovery, conquest, subjugation and enslavement of far away lands. Racial supremacy was used as a justification to enslave Africans in the American colonies during the Trans-Atlantic slave trade. This continued to happen until the abolition of slavery in Britain in 1807, across the British Empire in 1837.[17] In America, it was abolished with the Emancipation Proclamation in 1863.

The abolition of slavery only ended the practice of slavery. It didn't end racism itself, which by this stage had become institutionalised into the letter of the law across the United States and other Anglosphere countries, including Australia. It was commonplace for there to be laws segregating whites from blacks across different neighbourhoods, having access to separate public facilities, for restricting blacks from being hired in certain professions, for prohibiting intermarriages and even restricting immigration.

Fighting racism in the mid-1800s meant prioritising the abolition of slavery. That worked. Slavery is a thing of the past. Fighting racism in the mid-1900s meant prioritising the repeal of all such laws that discriminated against people based on race. That too worked. Inspired largely by the efforts of Civil Rights Era activists like Martin Luther King (Jnr) these laws began to be repealed in the 1950s and 1960s, with follow-on effects across the rest of the Anglosphere.

Australia had its own discriminatory laws at the time. Its immigration policy, the so-called White Australia Policy in 1901, restricted immigration based on a 'dictation test', the underlying motivation was to preserve

Australia's character as fundamentally British and to a lesser extent European society.[18] The other reasons were to prevent wages being undercut by those willing to work for less and to prevent the kinds of racial divisions already observable in America. Indigenous Australians could vote in federal elections if their state laws allowed them to. Queensland and Western Australia barred them until 1962. It took Australia until 1962 for the barriers to Indigenous voting in federal elections to be lifted. In 1967, they were counted as part of the population census and federal legislation could be created for them following a nation-wide referendum mandating these reforms with an almost 91% resounding majority.[19]

Yet now that institutions like slavery and discriminatory laws have been abolished, every time we hear present-day critics talking about eliminating racism, we have to ask, what should present-day struggles against perceived or actual racism even look like? This requires a closer look. The two main dimensions of the cultural debate over Australia's racism are historical disadvantage and present-day inequality. In the view of the left of politics, both of these are interdependent. On the other hand, those on the right claim the problem is more complex, with government largesse and paternalism, for instance, contributing in no small measure to poorer outcomes for Indigenous people. We can't deny what history shows: the historical disadvantage of Indigenous people by colonial settlers and, subsequently, colonial authorities. What we can and should question is whether acknowledging these historical realities can meaningfully impact the present-day policies and laws aimed at creating better opportunities for Indigenous communities. A line has to be drawn in the sand so that our acknowledgement of past injustices doesn't cause cultural paralysis, which would essentially undermine our sense of attachment to Australia. In fact, this remains a challenge for countries of the Anglosphere in general.

The example of Senator Lidia Thorpe's outburst in the Parliament, labelling the late Queen Elizabeth II as a 'coloniser' and refusing to take the Oath of Allegiance, is an acute example of the modern left's antagonism towards Australian history.[20] It is not enough to acknowledge the misdeeds of the past, but we must forever atone for them as a collective society. Resistance and aggressive rhetoric are, for the left, necessary adjuncts to ending racism in Australia. The focus of discussion, as such, becomes historical and backward looking rather than concrete forward looking policies for future generations. To acknowledge the problems associated with colonialism becomes a concession that Australia was built on racist foundations and can never be recovered from that, so its institutions need to be undermined and subverted, and that progress is only possible by fixating upon a guilt arising from centuries ago.

Rather than antagonism and cultural warfare, Australia needs leadership and vision to encourage its citizens to achieve aspirations not only as individuals, but as a broader community. The foundation for such aspiration needs to be shared hope, not guilt, and the protection of traditions, not the subversion of one in favour of another. In Doris Pilkington's famous Australian novel, *Rabbit Proof Fence,* she writes of the Noongar people, who had been dispossessed of their cultural traditions by colonialism:

> "[T]hese teachers and keepers of the traditional Law were prevented from practising it. They had to fight to find ways to return to their secret and sacred sites to perform their dances and other ceremonies that were crucial to their culture and whole way of life. Their pain and suffering remained hidden and repressed, silent and deep. They remembered the corroborees and songs that they were forbidden to dance and sing unless commanded by government officials. No longer would the corroborees be shared and danced by scores of feet, kicking up the dust in the moonlight around the glowing fires. Warriors with painted bodies and plumes of feathers on their ochre-covered heads would become faded images, buried in the past. The important dates on their seasonal calendars would be forgotten."[21]

The tragedy underlying Pilkington's evocative writing is the fact that culture is fragile and easily damaged, even erased. Traditions, whether Indigenous or non-Indigenous, can be, and have been, repressed, subverted and destroyed and the conservation of culture is often subjected to the influence of outside forces. We only need to look at recent history to find examples in other nation states, such as the founder of modern Turkey's Mustafa Kemal Atatürk who led a campaign to reform, modernise (or Westernise) and replace the education, dress codes, religious practices and almost every other aspect of Turkish society. In Communist China, historians tell us of Mao Zedong's Cultural Revolution, which aimed to 'cleanse' his party and Chinese society of certain traditions, superstitions and many of its ancient cultural practices in order to modernise the society in a short time period.[22] Whatever historical period we choose, we constantly find the erosion of cultural memory and tradition at the expense of progress, whether it is European imperialism in Australia or ideological revolutions elsewhere in the world.

So it is incumbent on Australians, of both Indigenous and non-Indigenous descents alike, to be on our guard against the erosion of cultural memory and tradition. Acknowledging the misdeeds of the past shouldn't hinder or subvert the collective attempts at preserving a shared Australian cultural heritage. It is possible to learn from our story, be proud of it and take responsibility for it. We can't simply pick and choose our story as so often is the case in political discourse, but we should use it as a reminder of where we came from and to plan a better future. The richness of the Noongar people's traditions should be conserved and celebrated alongside the richness of Australia's British heritage. Why are the two incompatible? Things like the rule of law, democracy and the freedom of expression form part of the fabric of Australian society as much as the stories of the Dreamtime, respect and guardianship of the country, the corroboree and many other Indigenous traditions.

If we constantly pit race against race or tradition against tradition, Australian society will come to resemble a shattered vision of what it could have been, rather than a unified vision of what it could be. Without a shared goal for our country, inequality, discrimination and antagonism become commonplace, attitudes that undermine progress, promote guilt and the obliteration of traditions and – most worryingly – angry clashes between citizens. To undermine the monarchy and label it a 'coloniser' is, today, more important than developing concrete proposals for preserving and promoting Indigenous traditions. To mount a sustained and coordinated campaign against the date of Australia Day seems to be more important than, for instance, investing in educational or health outcomes for remote communities. These are complex and difficult issues to solve yet whipping up outrage over a 'Change the Date' protest seems to provide some far more immediate satisfaction.

These symbolic and antagonistic attitudes too often rear their head in political environments, but for decades now, they have also become regular modes of thought in Australia's educational system. How can Australia develop better economic policies for Indigenous and non-Indigenous people across the country if politicians and teachers are too busy discussing the removal of the Australian flag, the changing of dates for Australia Day, or labelling the Monarch a 'coloniser'? National debates over Constitutional Recognition, racism, historical disadvantage, all have their place, but they too often become vehicles for such ideological and cultural hostilities to take root and distract from a shared and tangible goal. Without this, Australians will be unable to make true and durable progress into the future.

While the present is a continuation of the past, the trajectory is constantly subjected to upheavals and evolves rapidly. Its progression may seem linear, but what happens along the journey may be better represented as a zig zag rather than a straight line. Understanding these ebbs and flows gives us a richer appreciation of history. Australia has had a troubled past, without a doubt. It wasn't as troubled as some critics make it out to be, but it was troubled, full stop. No honest observer could deny that. As with most stories, there have been winners and losers in ours. Those left behind have gradually come to be lifted up and we're still far from achieving the best that we can on reconciliation. But we would struggle to do that by bringing down the social structures within which we exist. We must move forwards together while making these structures better each day. It's pivotal to this end, that our youth gets actively interested in thinking critically about the past.

As discussed, racism is a form of supremacism. It can be both a belief and a set of discriminatory actions against others. It isn't the only form of supremacism that exists in society. Often, the discrimination that takes place against individuals could have a basis in religion, sectarianism, ethnocentrism, nationalism, or even age, gender, class, or ability. The kind of uncultured racism where someone dislikes another *mainly* based on physical appearance is by and large a non-issue in modern Australian society. We have gotten into the habit of spending far more time discussing that kind of explicitly appearance-based racism than we perhaps need to. Australia has laws in place that combat racial discrimination. Not the least of which is the *Racial Discrimination Act* (1975). While critics might well argue that the existence of such legislation is proof that racism has been part and parcel of Australia's social fabric, this would be a one-sided view. Forms of supremacism both at the belief and practice levels do exist across most if not all world cultures and Australia is no exception. Yet the fact that Australia has passed such strict laws and kept them in place shows that the nation is naturally predisposed to fairness and equality. This is something we should continue to celebrate. Like any society, individuals in Australia can come with all sorts of attitudes, but Australia as a whole is not a racist country.

4

Was Australia built on 'stolen land'?

The most central question for Australia is whether or not the country was built on 'stolen land'. That's because the question is fraught with concerning implications for the future of this country. If we are on stolen land, then recognising this isn't the end of the debate. It's the beginning of round two, which leads us down a path of no recovery. Such a recognition essentially legitimises the cause to either decolonise this country as we know it and replace it with an Indigenous super-structure as a first preference. Or, to seek reparations to compensate for the 'land theft' as a second preference. Neither of these scenarios are outcomes the Australian public should want to see played out to their logical conclusions.

Yet despite its potential repercussions, there has been a lack of critical scrutiny on this stolen land accusation. Its advocates tend to endlessly repeat that we're built on 'stolen land' and that sovereignty was never ceded[23] as if these were uncontested facts. Its opponents usually end up getting offended and dismissing the accusation while launching personal attacks on the critic,[24] instead of presenting a logical counter-argument. This chapter gives the stolen land debate the scrutiny it deserves. It places the circumstances leading up to Australia's settlement at the forefront of our understanding. It thoroughly examines the nature of conquests throughout history in light of the evolving nature of global conventions and international law. It tries to reflect on the moral implications of British arrival in Australia. It presents a counter-argument to the underlying logic of the claim that Australia is a product of land theft.

To get started, it's crucial to note that open societies with democratic institutions do tend to produce criticism aimed at themselves. As with all things in life, some criticism might be legitimate, some half-legitimate and some altogether illegitimate. That's the nature of things. This 'stolen lands' idea is an outgrowth of this seemingly enlightened tendency. There are many societies in the world where the perceived and actual wrongdoings of past generations go unnoticed. As the Anglosphere's case has shown, there has been no shortage of criticism about past and present conducts of various governments and their policies. Most of this criticism has come out of Great Britain and the United States and is directed at them. This is unsurprising. One was a great colonial empire and the other has been a global military superpower since winning both World War I (1914-1918) and World War II (1939-1945). Both these facts make the two countries conveniently susceptible to a mixture of valid and invalid criticisms from within.

Although Australia is neither a military superpower nor a colonial empire, it does happen to be established by one – the British Empire. As such, Australia hasn't been exempt from receiving its share of criticism from sections of its own educated classes either. The suggestion that Australia was built on 'stolen land' has been around for many decades. Yet it has only begun to gain popularity in mainstream media in recent years. In particular, the decade since Prime Minister Kevin Rudd's Apology in 2008.[25] Even though media outlets only represent a negligible portion of the total population, they have the capacity to turn an idea into an orthodoxy by persistently broadcasting it over and over again. If repeated often enough, there eventually comes a time when the simulated idea starts to penetrate sections of public opinion.[26] In other words, that 'simulation' itself becomes the new reality so to speak, as French cultural theorist Jean Baudrillard argued in his 1981 treatise *Simulacra and Simulation*.[27] When ideas get popular, rightly or wrongly, the quest for truth can be compromised. People start to believe ideas to be true, not necessarily because they've weighed up the arguments for and against the idea on offer, but rather because subscribing to the idea has become the popular thing to do.

This is when we start to see celebrities jumping on bandwagons to mobilise their fans under the guise of supporting a 'higher cause'. Such moments should be seen as wake up calls, but rarely serve that purpose. On the contrary, ideas that become popular through mass repetition by famous people can result in a mass psychosis in human societies. With a shift in public opinion comes a shift in political outcomes. Although the thought of a psychosis is less frightening when the idea going around happens to be something we agree with. If, on the other hand, the idea is objectionable, we start to feel that people are being brainwashed. What has just been described here has more or less been the media landscape around this stolen land debate, as well as with other ancillary issues that may arise out of the original debate. We see activists advocating to change the date of Australia Day.[28] This is a classic example of an ancillary debate that has arisen out of an earlier debate. If it's established that Australia was built on 'stolen land' then what's the point of having a national holiday to celebrate the exact day on which this alleged 'land theft' took place? It makes perfect sense from the point of view of those who actually believe we are on stolen land to then advocate to change the date.

There are many more examples of activists making demands to edit the default settings of our national 'branding'. Consider the demands to recognise Indigenous Australians in the Constitution,[29] to sign a Treaty,[30] or more recently, to establish what has been described as a Voice to Parliament.[31] These are the sorts of measures being sought by a vocal minority of activists who believe they're doing the right thing. The underlying basis for these demands is that this land shouldn't have been colonised in the first place, sovereignty was never ceded, the British Empire was a 'racist' foreign regime that has got away with doing all these nasty things to the original inhabitants of this land, so you now owe us. That's more or less what these measures are — reparations masquerading as reconciliation. On one level, we have to admire the moral fortitude with which many activists have committed themselves to this cause. Just as one can disagree with socialism while respecting the fact that socialists are generally those who wish to seek a fairer society, one could appreciate that those who tend to push for measures like the Voice to Parliament are generally decent, well-intentioned Australians. It just happens to be the case that conservatives see the issue differently. That doesn't mean that either side is arguing in bad faith.

Australia has managed to arrive at this junction for reasons some keen observers of the nation's political landscape from the time of the Mabo Decision (1992) always feared from the beginning. Yet we're at this tipping point because there hasn't been a concerted effort to push back against the social forces that led us here. Their arguments haven't been properly challenged and refuted in the eyes of the public. Instead, our society has become more punitive towards those going against established orthodoxies, even where that works to our own detriment. Add to this, the fact that our youth finds history 'boring' and enrolments in high school history subjects are flatlining nationally and struggling to attract new students.[32] As discussed in earlier chapters we, as present-day observers, have an indispensable relationship with the past. The world we live in is a direct product of things that happened in timeframes before ours. The discovery and settlement of Australia is an event that each of us, who calls Australia home, is deeply connected with.

This makes it impossible to just sit back and ignore this stolen land debate. To put things in perspective, it is no secret that this island continent was already inhabited long before European contact by disparate Indigenous tribes who maintained a nomadic lifestyle. From roaming the deserts, to the coastline, to river valleys, to mountains to the bush, these tribes moved around freely, based on necessity. Indigenous Australians developed advanced navigation techniques using which they could trek their way through this vast island continent in harsh climatic conditions. This remains an impressive story of adaptation and survival. Equally, it is no secret that this place began to attract successive waves of European explorers from 1606 onwards, with Dutchman Captain Willem Janszoon being the first to reach what we now call the Gulf of Carpentaria in between the two iconic peaks on Australia's map.[33] Then came the Englishman William Dampier who began charting the coast of Western Australia in 1688.[34] Following waves of successive European explorers in between, the explorer who got to claim the land on behalf of an actual empire was the Englishman from Yorkshire, Captain James Cook in 1770.[35]

Not long after this, the British Empire would be plunged into the greatest catastrophe it wasn't expecting and didn't need – the American Revolution. Those American colonies served more than a single vital purpose for the British Empire. Prisons across Britain were generally overcrowded in those days and the idea of deporting convicts to remote colonies far from Britain itself had become a very attractive idea. After the Americans were taxed by King George III without direct parliamentary representation, this became one of the chief grievances that would inspire a revolt against British rule. Although the revolutionary wars went on from 1775 to 1783, the original American 13 colonies declared their independence on 4th July 1776.[36] Britain's military efforts to regain control over the lost territories carried on until 1815 but were unsuccessful for the most part.

Canada remained under British control, but it was expected that it would be moving towards eventual independence from Britain, which did end up being granted in 1867.[37] This was all happening at a time when British prisons continued to remain overcrowded.[38] With the loss of the American colonies, combined with the possibility of Canada too going its own way, the conditions were ripe for the British Empire to start looking elsewhere in search of new penal colonies. Following the Battle of Plassey in 1757, parts of the Subcontinent had begun falling under the rule of the British East India Company,[39] except that wouldn't have been ideal to establish a penal colony. The region was too densely populated with a diverse local population with its own customs, traditions, beliefs and languages dating back thousands of years. The locals wouldn't have taken kindly to the local demography being radically altered by a disproportionate influx of British convicts, nor for that matter, free settlers, in the midst of their society.

Australia had already been claimed for the British Empire by Captain James Cook earlier in 1770 and was available at its disposal. Based on his journal entries from earlier voyages, the British inferred that the island continent was a giant piece of land — except, sparsely populated. It was understood, there was no central government with which to negotiate. Its native population was largely nomadic and at a different stage of economic development in comparison to some of the other local populations the empire had previously encountered. It was against this backdrop that the decision to start settling Australia as a penal colony came about. By coming to terms with this justification, we can already see how little of it was a case of conquest out of blatant greed for land as a means to spread Western civilisation, as is often presumed by critics. Following on from a decision born out of necessity, the First Fleet arrived in 1788 after 18 years from the moment the region was first claimed for the British Crown.[40]

It is important to reflect on the immediate aftermath of the start of settlement. This would enable us to assess whether any part of the exchange between British settlers and Indigenous tribesmen indicates a scenario that resembles 'land theft'. New South Wales became the first penal colony to be established. As intended, the island continent of Australia soon became fertile ground for attracting thousands of convicts. At last, the British Empire had found a replacement for the lost colonies in America. The practice of convict transportation went on from the moment of the First Fleet's arrival in 1788 until the last convict ship docked at the port of Fremantle in Western Australia in 1868.[41] As it happens, both during the convict period and after it, thousands of free settlers who weren't convicts also ended up choosing to settle in Australia from the British Isles in search of a new life. It was this interaction between the convicts, free settlers, workers from other backgrounds, Indigenous tribes and British officials here to govern on behalf of the Crown that gradually helped forge our unique Australian national identity and way of life.

The level of harmony between British settlers and native Indigenous tribes varied depending on location, time and circumstance. There is no generic trend here that can be objectively proven. Historians such as Henry Reynolds have carefully documented acts of Indigenous resistance to colonialism since settlement. It is indefensible to say that the two communities always got along like a house on fire. But, it is equally indefensible to say that the two communities were mostly at war with each other. It has become common for countless present-day observers to grab one of these two opposing positions and start talking it up with absolute certainty. While events such as the 'massacre' of Pinjarra in Western Australia or the so-called 'Black War' in Tasmania are frequently cited by some as major examples of colonial aggression against Indigenous people, almost no attention is paid to *successful* interactions between the Europeans and native cultures.

In New South Wales, for instance, Governor Macquarie established a school for Indigenous children in 1814, leading to one Indigenous girl winning first prize in the school board examinations ahead of European students. In 1868, the first all-Indigenous cricket team toured England with impressive results, leading one English fast bowler, George Tarrant, to praise one of the Indigenous batsmen, proclaiming: "I have never bowled to a better batsman."[42] These are, of course, simply hand-picked examples, but they serve to illustrate a complicated dynamic at play between European and Indigenous cultures in Australia, one far more interesting than oversimplified arguments about 'massacre' and 'conquest'. As discussed earlier, the role of a professional historian is to go by primary source evidence that has been carefully interpreted before drawing conclusions or making judgements about what happened in the past. Even then, there is an undeniable element of human frailty. This is why extraordinary claims should be treated with a grain of salt, unless the evidence is compelling beyond doubt. The reality is that the initial encounters between Brits and natives were a mixed bag. There was a combination of both harmony and confrontations.

It's clear by now that the decision to settle Australia was born out of the need for abundant space to transport convicts after losing the American colonies and Britain itself having overcrowded prisons. For those interested in exploring other factors behind the decision to settle Australia, some of which may even shift the emphasis away from the need for a penal colony may wish to explore famous historian Geoffrey Blainey's *The Tyranny of Distance* first published in 1966.[43] It is interesting to note that those who believe Australia to be built on stolen land also view it as a racist country. While the racism question has been dealt with in a separate chapter, it's almost impossible to find a critic who believes Australia to be a product of 'land theft' but doesn't think Australia is a racist country as well. The two viewpoints go hand in hand. From the critic's viewpoint, if the land was stolen while knowing it was already inhabited by a much older culture dating back 60,000 years, then that automatically implies those British settlers would have to have been racist to native Indigenous communities. Why else would they ignore Indigenous presence on this land and proceed to start settling it without sovereignty being ceded, as we're often reminded?

This makes it important to reflect on the initial few decades of Australia's settlement as far as race relations were concerned. It's a gross exaggeration to suggest, as some often do, that the entirety of the 1800s was fraught with clashes and genocide. There has never been uncontested proof of any official government policy of mass genocide by the British towards native Indigenous tribes. If anything, there are many notable instances where members of the two communities maintained cordial terms. The story of Woollarawarre Bennelong is a prime example. He was the first known Indigenous Australian to have managed to forge a friendship with the authorities of the day.[44] He was taken to England to meet King George III. Having learnt English, Bennelong often played a key role in negotiations between British settlers and Indigenous people. The standard criticism about a stolen land built by racists would suggest a lack of good will between the two communities, which is exaggerated. There was good will and mutual cooperation. Australians who follow politics might recall 25th Prime Minister John Howard as the Federal Member for 'Bennelong' between 1974 and 2007. That's right, Howard's seat was named after the same bloke we've just discussed.

Following settlement, this island continent would go on to be made up of various self-governing British colonies. Originally, these colonies reported directly to the British Crown, but grew to be more independent over time and established their own local Parliaments to pass local laws. Through the influx of convicts until 1868 and free settlers, a unique culture and way of life was already beginning to take shape by the middle of that century. Meanwhile, industrialisation across China and Japan following European and American pressures had essentially led the two ancient civilisations to develop imperial ambitions of their own in order to stay competitive in global power play and trade. China and Japan had seen the behaviour of European imperial powers and the rapid rate at which empires from Britain, Portugal, Spain, France, Italy and Russia among others had managed to acquire large amounts of land across the Americas, Africa and Asia. Chinese and Japanese leadership in those days felt it was time to play catch up.

Australia had experienced the discovery of gold in the colony of Victoria in 1851 in a period known as the Gold Rush.[45] This attracted many free settlers to the region in search of employment, not only from the British Isles but also from other parts of the British Empire, China and various islands in the Pacific Ocean. The initial experience between Australians of European ancestry and Chinese workers hadn't always resulted in communal harmony. The willingness of the Chinese to work longer hours at cheaper rates made their hiring quite attractive to employers. There were growing concerns that Chinese presence in Australia in the middle of the 1800s was driving wages down and putting Australians of European ancestry out of work. There were often clashes between Australian and Chinese workers. Present-day critics sometimes weaponise this part of our past to suggest that Australia is in fact a 'racist' country. But a racist country wouldn't have allowed workers of a different race to gain entry with an intention to work in the first place.

While clashes and general disharmony between any two communities is altogether undesirable in any day and age, the economic motivations behind this instance can't be ignored. When Europeans attempted to make contact with the Chinese under the Qing dynasty's reign around the same time, the Chinese didn't always look favourably upon working with Europeans for a mixture of valid and invalid reasons. People can be inherently suspicious of outsiders, especially in the middle of the 1800s – the global heyday of imperialism. Anyone who had the capability to raise an army and conquer their neighbours more or less did so without thinking twice. Besides, the occasional disharmony that came about within colonial Australia in the 1800s didn't just limit itself to Europeans versus Chinese. If anything, there are more accounts of Europeans versus Europeans. The Castle Hill Rebellion in 1804 is a classic example of this. A group of Irishmen revolted and attempted to escape back to Ireland.[46] The revolt was ultimately crushed. A similar example was in 1810 with the Rum Rebellion where Governor of New South Wales William Bligh faced a revolt and was eventually replaced.

The crucial point is that clashes were a feature of the political and economic realities of, what was, a harsh timeframe to be around. As discussed, the most frequent form in which clashes took place was between Europeans of different stripes. It would be anachronistic to interpret the disharmony with the Chinese through the lens of modern concepts of racism. It would almost sound like we're suggesting that when clashes took place in the 1800s between let's say two lots of English or Irish settlers, that's not racist, but if the same thing involves non-Europeans then that's automatically racist. That's how some think and it makes little sense. It clouds our judgement and prevents us from being able to get a balanced perspective on our past. Growing anxieties about Chinese and Japanese imperial ambitions abroad and clashes with Chinese workers at home, combined with the fact that Australia had, by the second half of the 1800s, come to develop its own unique identity and way of life as an improved version of working class British culture, all of these factors created the requisite conditions for those disparate British colonies of this island continent to come together under a federated arrangement and become a nation-state of our own. This is what happened in 1901 when the Commonwealth of Australia appeared on the world map and embraced a restrictive immigration policy to ensure its cultural self-preservation.

As discussed in earlier chapters, this book is not to be read as a history book. Its job is not to bring to us a descriptive account of everything that happened following the settlement of Australia. There exists an abundance of peer-reviewed academic literature on the history bookshelf offering a variety of viewpoints. The purpose of this book — and more specifically this chapter — is something far more crucial than that. To refresh our memories, the aim here is to specifically look at that oft-repeated charge that 'racist' Australia was built on 'stolen land'. To assist our inquiry, what we have done so far is to trace the sequence of events between the British Empire's decision to settle Australia in 1788 until the independent colonies became a Federation in 1901. The 1800s was the century that defined Australia's culture, identity and way of life. In taking a look at select defining moments within this period, we have dispelled a few common myths. The decision to settle had less to do with territorial greed and more to do with the need for a new penal colony after the loss of the American colonies in 1776.

We have so far discussed how relations between British settlers and Indigenous people were a mixed bag. We have discussed how there was no official policy of institutionalised genocide. We have discussed how clashes between Australians and the Chinese weren't unique to racial differences. We discussed how similar, if not worse, clashes were also taking place between different varieties of *European* settlers, such as the Irish. We have discussed how China and Japan's newfound imperial ambitions had become a source of anxiety for Australia as a new nation in the process of finding its own identity. In comparison to the vast majority of world societies, this social and political backdrop of early Australia in the 1800s sounds less racist, less elitist and less hostile. The revolts were minor. The clashes didn't last long. The cross-cultural exchange was relatively harmonious despite being a mixed bag. The account of settlement didn't take place through any act of war, let alone resistance by the natives. There are far more aggressive and institutionally racist accounts of European takeover of other lands, most notably by the Spanish and the Portuguese across North and South Americas. We discussed how this wasn't the case with the British in Australia.

The next stage of the discussion comes down evaluating the criteria by which land ownership can be determined. This isn't a case of determining the ownership of a house within a jurisdiction where the governing force is property law. We're talking about state rights. In the realm of nationhood and state-formation, conventional laws of private property don't apply. It's a separate ball game altogether. This needs a bit of thought. It's crucial to point out here what may seem obvious enough to jurists, lawyers and other thinkers, but not so obvious outside those professions. There is a difference between morality and legality. What is legal isn't always moral. What is moral isn't always legal.

The idea of 'theft' in general is defined as claiming ownership of something that belongs to someone else. If we find something that has no owner and decide to keep it, that's not the same as taking something despite the knowledge that it has an owner. Theft is universally wrong. There is a range of laws that are completely arbitrary, for instance, the age at which a person may drink alcohol or buy cigarettes. If one was on an uncharted island out at sea, one is technically outside of any nation-state's jurisdiction. If a minor drinks alcohol in such a place, it would be difficult, if not impossible, to ascertain which country's laws were being broken. To be more imaginative, the same would apply on board a satellite station floating in space. But theft is theft no matter where it takes place. It is basically a moral issue, which just happens to take on legal forms in literally every jurisdiction. Suffice it to say, the relationship between morals and laws isn't always as perfectly consistent as that.

Humans have always been known to move around. We are what biologists may describe as migratory species. In other words, we go where necessity takes us. Irrespective of whether we take a creationist view or an evolutionist view of where it all began, one thing that's clear is that humans have always moved around from one place to another out of necessity. This continues to be the case today. If we go by the creationist view, then Adam and Eve started out somewhere in the ancient Middle East, their descendants right down to Noah's three sons Ham, Shem and Japheth went and settled different ends of the earth and became the forefathers of the diverse range of modern humans over centuries. During the early modern period, many Orientalists attributed the differences in human physical appearances to descent from different sons of Noah. If we go by the evolutionist view, then we evolved from single cell organisms to multiple cell organisms, hopped out of the water, became land creatures, got divided into different biological varieties due to natural selection, from which came primates who developed bi-pedalism, from which came the australopithecines to neanderthals to homo sapiens sapiens, which is us modern humans.

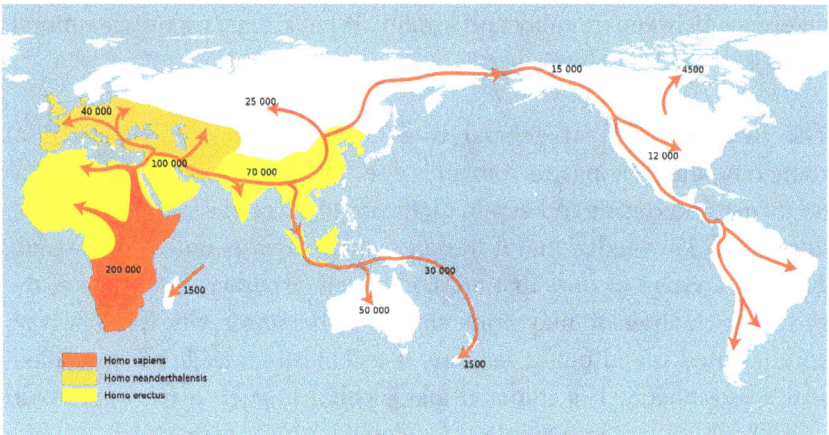

(Source: Wikimedia Commons)

Humans have moved around from one place to another in search of a better life. As can be seen from this map, Indigenous Australians also came to settle in Australia some 50,000 to 60,000 years ago. Back then, the search for a better life meant finding the perfect living conditions, livable climate, fertile soils, resourceful plants and animals at the very least that would make it suitable for hunting, gathering and farming. While there were no international borders that demarcated one ethnic nation's land from the rest, geographical terrain such as rivers, mountains, valleys, forests and deserts tended to act as natural barriers that demarcated one community of humans from another in the ancient times. As different people settled in different geographical territories, they developed their own distinct languages, dialects, writing scripts and ways of life. Narrowing down the sample space within which marriages and births would take place, combined with dietary choices relative to specific topological realities resulted in diversity in human appearances. All of these factors combined became the defining features of identification for the development of 'ethnicities' and 'nations' as political constructs.

It's difficult to think of a single region in the world that has ever been reserved for the exclusive use of a single variety of humans. The vast majority of world territories have been home to multiple ethnicities and nationalities at various stages of their development. That is the lens through which Indigenous and British presence on the island continent of Australia should be seen. As far as governance was concerned, from the advent of early city-states some 5,000 years ago until the rise of nationalism only a couple of centuries ago, most societies were governed by empires.[47] These were very large multi-ethnic and multi-linguistic entities that generally came about as the result of territorial expansionism through war. It is true that in our times, we generally frown upon the idea of war. We see this frowning as the hallmark of civilised society. But this mode of thinking that shuns war doesn't represent the bulk of human history. Winning a war used to be considered the highest form of political achievement.

Anyone that was capable of commanding an army and going to war with an intention to raid, pillage, plunder and capture new lands, did so. No major civilisation in the world has been exempt from this activity. In terms of how much land a particular regime was able to conquer depended on a variety of factors. The strength of the military itself was far from the primary, let alone sole factor. Often, a regime's capacity to expand depended upon the shape of its own geography. As we look at which major European powers managed to colonise the Americas, we find names like Portugal, Spain, France and Britain as the four prominent colonisers of the continents of North and South America. As far as that specific pattern of territorial expansion is concerned, what each of these powers had in common was that the regime was headquartered in Western Europe, right on the seabeds of the Atlantic Ocean. Becoming a great naval power came naturally. All these regimes had to do was sail west.

As we look at regimes that were situated more in-land across continental Europe, we find little proof of comparable colonial activity. German colonialism for instance, simply couldn't keep up with its Western European counterparts. Germany did hone in on what is known as the Scramble for Africa in the late 1800s, which was a period when European imperial powers turned towards the African continent to set up more colonies.[48] But there was never any German equivalent of what Argentina was to Spain, or Australia to Britain, or Quebec to France – mirror images of one's own society implanted thousands of kilometres away from home. There was no lack of military capacity or technological innovation on the part of Germany, but its unique geography prevented it from gaining seamless naval passage to sail across and compete with the rest of the Western European powers.

Russia's case is yet more peculiar. As Russia was even further to the east with no access to any warm water ports, it never really managed to become a major naval superpower. Although it did look east to launch on a massive land-based expansionist campaign across several centuries. As a result, Russia today remains the largest country by territorial size out of all. Territorial expansion hasn't been limited to European powers either. Relative to the availability of technological means and capacity to travel long distances, most major civilisations that had the capacity to spread out as far as they could in search of new lands and resources did so. The rise and spread of Islamic civilisation in the 600s CE is a prime example. Starting out in the deserts of the Arabian Peninsula, early Muslim armies not only managed to conquer the entire peninsula and later marched on to conquer sizeable chunks of the known world at the time.[49] At one point, Islamic civilisation's diverse empires stretched from Spain in the west to China in the east.

In the process of its territorial expansion, many existing regimes collapsed and were substituted with Muslim regimes. Many existing ethnicities and nations were transformed and their local identities morphed into the newfound culture. Arabic became the *lingua franca* of the bulk of these lands. Yet neither is any of this activity seen as 'imperialism' or 'colonialism' by present-day critics, nor is it seen as a case of societies built on 'stolen land'. It hardly even features in most public discussions. In the rare instance when it does, early Islamic territorial expansion is seen as consistent with the social and political norms of the timeframe in which it took place. It is also seen as a series of gradual territorial gains resulting from retaliations when under attack from neighbouring powers. It has been established so far that conquests were neither considered immoral nor unlawful for the most part of world history. Every culture and society that had the means to expand its dominions did so, by whatever means available. Recall our examples from earlier about the importance of geography in shaping political destinies.

While conquering was everyone's game, in the past five centuries or so Europeans have played it better. In the process, various European regimes ended up conquering and setting up overseas colonies on virtually every continent of the planet. By the time the 1900s came around, there was no square centimetre of the world left uncharted that hadn't at some point had the flag of a European imperial power hoisted on its soil. The only exceptions where countries weren't conquered and settled was when two imperial powers decided to leave a buffer in between, so as to not end up too close for comfort on each other's borders. The British and the French did this with Thailand – left it alone – because the French were in Vietnam then known as Indo-China, and the Brits were in the Subcontinent. It helped to not share a border with each other where possible in case that led to clashes. The Russians and the British did this with Afghanistan as a buffer separating out British-ruled Subcontinent from Russian-ruled Central Asia.

The European age of exploration is generally frowned upon by present-day critics. It's presumed that most of the world's economic, political and social problems in developing countries are to be blamed on colonialism. It's understandably disturbing for some that European powers came, saw, conquered, supposedly or actually uprooted local cultures, inadvertently ended up introducing a bunch of diseases to which native populations had no immunity and ended up destroying Indigenous ways of life, replacing them with European super-structures. None of the colonialism from other civilisations are scrutinised to the same scale. One of the reasons for this is that most of Europe's conquests are more recent. By comparison, most early Islamic conquests came about during the 600s and roughly the thousand year period that followed on from that. The last major attempt made by the Ottomans to penetrate mainland Europe was at the Battle of Vienna in 1683 which resulted in decisive victory for the Hapsburg dynasty and its alliance with Poland-Lithuania.[50] There were some wars fought by the Ottomans in and around eastern Europe after this, but these weren't noteworthy efforts to conquer more land in Europe. This reinforces the earlier point that in the recent 500 or so years, it's Europe that has dominated the quest for territorial expansion.

Since Europe stands accused of having 'stolen' more land than any other civilisation, it's again important to look at the circumstances that brought about the European age of exploration. Following on from the hunter-gather age, all organised societies have tended to rely on trade to survive. What isn't available in one region can be imported in. What isn't available in another region can be exported out. The Subcontinent was known for its spices in the Middle Ages.[51] Bear in mind, in those days there were no fridges and refrigerators as we have them. The only way to keep food stocks preserved for prolonged periods of time was by using spices from the Subcontinent as a recipe for prolonging shelf life. China was known for its porcelain, silk and polyester. Caravans of European merchants and tradesmen were initially able to take the trek by land along the famous Silk Route connecting Europe with the Subcontinent and China. Between 1095 and 1291 European Crusaders and Ottoman Turks went to a series of wars against each other over who gets to control Jerusalem. After initial blows, the Turks managed to hold on to the city — central to Jewish, Christian and Muslim traditions.

To safeguard Jerusalem from being invaded again, the Ottoman Turks felt they needed to keep European merchants as far away from the region as possible in case they were there to gather intelligence to plan a re-conquest. So to make the European journey to the Subcontinent and China as disincentivising as possible via the land routes, the Ottomans decided to impose a heavy tariff on all incoming European traffic passing through. The trick worked. This kicked off a long and serious debate among the European ruling elites about the need for an alternative route to get to the Subcontinent and China. There was some speculation in elite circles that there might be a so-called northwest passage to get to the east by travelling west. Whether or not the world was a sphere wasn't common knowledge for everyone in those days. Yet Genoan-born explorer Christopher Columbus was convinced that if the Europeans sailed west, they could find that or similar passage to by-pass the Ottoman Turks and get to the Subcontinent and China in the east.

In 1492, Columbus was commissioned to sail west by the Catholic Monarchs King Ferdinand II of Aragon and Queen Isabella I of Castile. His voyage did manage to find exotic lands, but not the spice-rich Subcontinent or silk-rich China that he was searching for. He had landed in what we now call the continent of North America, specifically the country now known as Bahamas. This has been the single most defining moment in early modern history. While the Europeans didn't find the north-west passage to get to the east, the entirely serendipitous discovery of this 'New World' as the two Americas, north and south, came to be known, brought many other economic, social, cultural and political benefits for various European powers. It didn't take long before other Western European powers joined the party and started setting up colonies. This bizarre new world was full of its own new products like tobacco, chocolate, maple syrup, potatoes, tomatoes and chilli peppers among other commodities which the Europeans had developed a fondness for. The new world had now become an attractive frontier to keep conquering and settling. By the end of 1492 when the age of exploration started, several colonial empires had begun expanding, relative to their geographies and navigational capabilities as shown on this map.

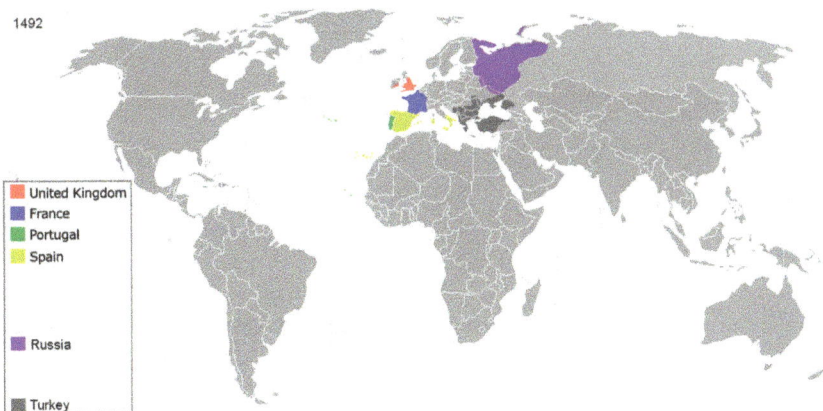

(Source: Wikimedia Commons)

The new world was the gift European powers couldn't have dreamt of. Spain at the time had a rigid system of inheritance called primogeniture which meant that the eldest got everything and other siblings were often left penniless. The more lands that the Spanish Empire now conquered across the Americas, the more attractive it became for ordinary Spanish folks who had missed out on the inheritance to sail west for a chance to be a landowner. For the next few centuries, European imperial powers would compete with each other militarily over control of new territories and resources, as well as with any native populations that got in the way of their pursuits. There were economic motivations behind this wave of exploration and colonisation, such as the need to find new markets, new commodities and trade. Additionally, there were religious motivations too that provided an overarching veneer of justification for the various acts of conquering (or 'stealing') new lands that were already inhabited by others. As far as they were concerned, if it was being done for God, then it vindicates the conquerors. They could say they were doing it all to convert and save the heathen populations in the newfound territories.

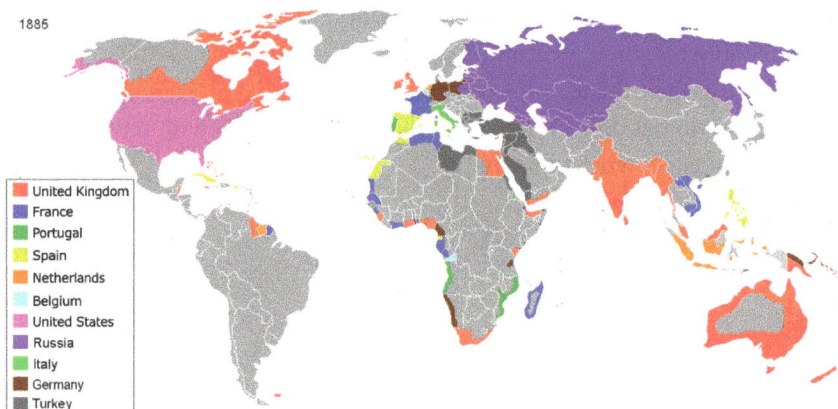

(Source: Wikimedia Commons)

Through the passage of time, more European powers who had the means to explore and conquer did so, where geography and political capacity permitted the building of powerful navies to sail across and land armies to fight wars against their rivals. As is clear by this stage, the age of European imperialism didn't start out of a vacuum. It had its own unique triggers, the need for trade met with Ottoman tariffs by the land route. We can see how serendipity led to the discovery of the Americas with new trading markets, new products to introduce to Europe and the ability to start fresh as a landowner if one was prepared to move across to the new world. As England decided to come to the party, it began establishing its own colonies in the north-eastern portion of the land. These are the colonies where convicts were previously sent along with free settlers and which, over a century or so, would go on to forge their own identity and eventually seek their independence from the British Empire. This is the backdrop that stimulated the need for Australia to be settled, or 'stolen' as per the accusation we are examining in this chapter.

What we have just finished discussing is how it used to be normal to go conquering lands. This wasn't just limited to European regimes. Others had done the same thing too for centuries, it's just that Europeans got better at playing that game over time for reasons that go beyond the scope of this book, but remains a fascinating inquiry in itself. We have also discussed the serendipitous nature of the material benefits of European imperialism starting in 1492. We discussed the specific reasons for Australia's settlement in 1788 and the mixed bag account of race relations until Australia became an independent Commonwealth in 1901. We have reflected on the distinction between legality, morality and privately owned property as opposed to land ownership as part of a nation-state. We're now ready to get stuck right into determining what is and isn't 'stolen land'. Recall the example from earlier that laws apply within jurisdictions. Whether something is illegal or not depends on what codified laws exist within a corresponding jurisdiction with an enforcement mechanism. The natural question arises, in what jurisdiction does the interaction outside of territorial jurisdictions take place? If there is no jurisdiction, then what's stopping one country from invading and conquering another? What laws could be used to stop such a thing from happening? So first we must approach this question from a purely legal standpoint, then a moral one.

For most of human history, there had never been a jurisdiction regulating the interaction that took place between different regimes. The vast majority of times, there were no rules of engagement. It was a world governed by a form of social Darwinism, or survival of the fittest. Sometimes, to get around this, some regimes would tend to establish their own conventions or mutual agreements, or voluntary treaties with their neighbours. If two dynasties fought each other off on a battlefield, whether they decided to release their prisoners of war or execute them on the spot depended entirely on the conventions that may have been prevalent in that specific timeframe and the overall nature of the relationship between the belligerent parties.

If the two had signed a treaty beforehand that said that if conflict broke out, we would act humane towards each other, then chances are such an arrangement would've been honoured. But the whole point is that in most instances, there were no treaties. It was more or less rules of the jungle. What that world never had was a written set of laws, or a geopolitical equivalent of Moses carrying the Stone Tablets with the Ten Commandments inscribed on them governing relations between territorial communities. There has never been any equivalent system that says a particular piece of land is reserved for the exclusive use of a single group of people where any conquerors or violaters of sovereignty would be punished.

This is why strong armies weren't just necessary for conquest, they were also necessary for self-defence. You may not be the warmonger, but what if the King from the village next door was and he decided to invade and make your village part of his dominion. Which court of appeal could you refer your complaint to? None. That's why strong militaries were necessary. The default mindset was that one had to conquer, or be conquered. Sitting on the fence wasn't an option. If you weren't actively out conquering, that meant it was only a matter of time before another army would be at your doorstep. It's understandable that we, as modern folks, wouldn't want to live in a world like this, but it shouldn't be too difficult for us to realise that that's how things worked back then because we've seen it all portrayed in so many famous films based on a mixture of actual and fictional historic themes. Take some notable examples from the past three decades: *Braveheart* (1995), *The Patriot* (2000), *Master and Commander* (2003), *The Last Samurai* (2003), *Alexander* (2004), *Troy* (2004), *Kingdom of Heaven* (2005), *300* (2006) and *Apocalypto* (2006).[52] The historic accuracy of these films may be a subject of debate but what they have done is a good job of capturing the essence of the social and political norms of the timeframes in which their stories are set. Precisely due to the luxury of having access to modern cinema, one doesn't need a PhD in history to realise that the glorification of war as the ultimate symbol of bravery and heroism was once the norm. The Australia we all live in – in 2023 – at the time of writing this book, isn't part of that world. We see war as a measure of last, rather than first resort. Yet the Australia that began to be settled in 1788 was the product of a completely different world where different norms applied. Looking at past norms through the lens of present norms doesn't always work.

This *everyone-vs-everyone* and *might-makes-right* type of a landscape didn't come to an end overnight. Across different timeframes, there have been attempts to establish some kind of rules to minimise the risk of war and save lives. The reality is, pretty much most such attempts didn't really achieve what their pioneers had hoped for. The Treaty of Westphalia in 1648 is one notable example. It came at the end of the Thirty Years War (1616-1648) which was a period of intense fighting between the German-speaking Protestant Kingdom of Bohemia with its allies on one side and the German-speaking Catholic Habsburg dynasty and its allies on the other. The point of the Treaty of Westphalia was to negotiate demarcated territories. It was the first attempt in relatively recent history to stop borders from constantly shrinking and expanding based on the haphazard outcomes of perpetual warfare. The concept of fixed borders meant that different regimes would respect each other's sovereignty. While this was a noble attempt, that treaty didn't really achieve much. It never even succeeded in putting an end to future wars.

The second such attempt was arguably what's known as the Congress of Vienna from 1814 to 1815.[53] It coincided with the end of the Napoleonic wars, specifically signed nine days before the Battle of Waterloo (1815). Again, the idea was noble and the execution reasonable enough. Except in the long run, it too had no real impact. War has always been a tragic feature of humanity's story. In particular, Europe's story. Like Westphalia, Vienna too resulted in nothing permanent in terms of enforcing respect for mutual sovereignty between nations. The entirety of the 1800s period was full of wars, revolutions, riots, revolts and civil wars. A series of revolutions that swept across Europe known as the European Spring in 1848 only helped create further chaos and collapsed several existing regimes.[54] As a side note, the term 'Arab Spring' widely used to describe the series of protests that swept many countries across North Africa and the Middle East from 2011 onwards is seen as a spin-off of the 'European Spring' of 1848. To return to the main point, to those within and outside of Europe, this specific century – the 1800s – also features some major defining wars. The Crimean War (1953-1856), the American Civil War (1861-1865), the Spanish-American War (1898) are notable examples. Europe's various empires had by this point outlived their own expectations and some might argue, grown larger than they could handle. This map shows the lay of the land as the world entered the 1900s – the twentieth century, that is.

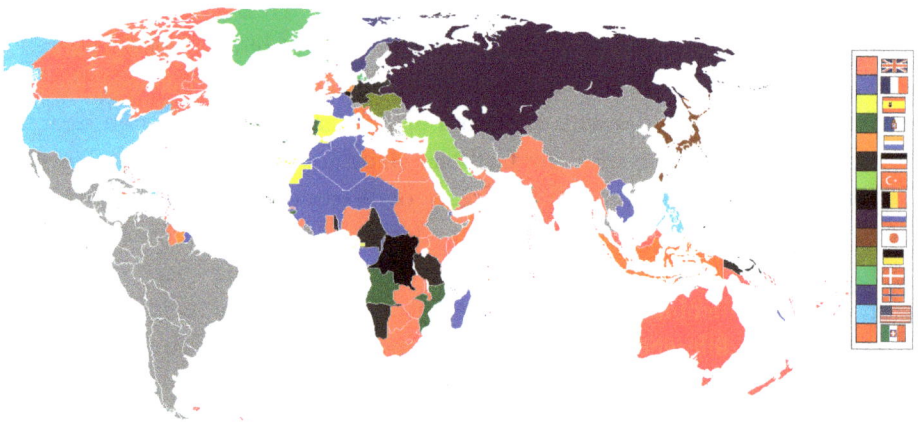

(Source: Wikimedia Commons)

There was, by this stage, no corner of the earth that hadn't fallen to one European imperial regime or another. Eventually World Wars I (1914-1918) and World Wars II (1939-1945) came around. Various European dynasties collapsed during the first of these. The interwar period was one of economic difficulty all over the world. By the second great war came to an end, the United States and the Soviet Union had emerged as the two major global superpowers vying for more influence, looking to set up puppet regimes all over the world, aligned to their interests. Each attempted to neutralise the other's growing influence by hook or crook. Meanwhile, the rest of the great European powers began to lose their overseas colonies through a process widely described as decolonisation. The Italians had left Libya by 1943. The Brits and the French had left Libya by 1951. Following a long and gruesome war, the French left Algeria in 1962. The Brits left the Subcontinent in 1947 leaving behind not one but two independent nation-states, a Muslim majority Pakistan and a Hindu majority India. They also left the British Mandate of Palestine, where the proposed United Nations Partition Plan 181 didn't work, war ensued between Zionist and Arab forces, and the modern State of Israel declared its independence. Countries continued to emerge on the world map through the rise of nationalism and former colonies would be vacated. The handover of Hong Kong from Britain to China in 1997 was the most recent notable example of decolonisation.

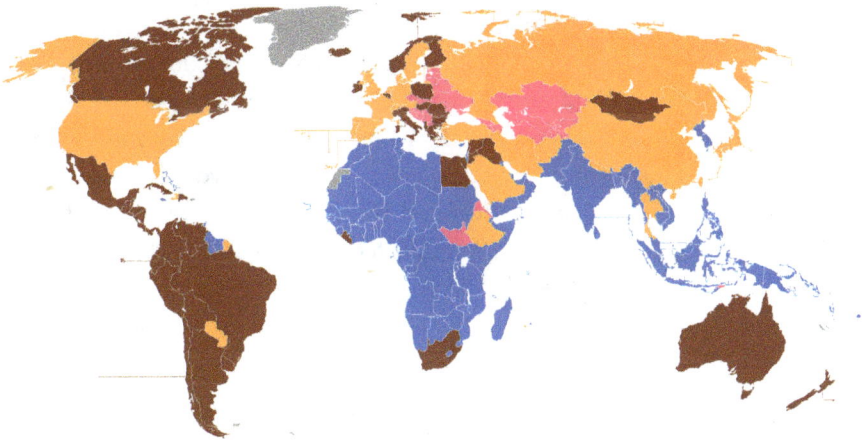

(Source: Wikimedia Commons)

To recap, the process of European expansionism began in 1492 and by the eve of World War I in 1914, meant that European powers controlled the majority of the world, with their overseas colonies on virtually every continent. Then, through multiple waves of decolonisation (as shown on the map above, began to vacate these colonies. Unlike America's case, Australia never had to win its independence over Great Britain through war. It was granted to us when we became a Federation in 1901 as discussed earlier. Given that neither the Treaty of Westphalia (1648) nor the Congress of Vienna (1814-1815) were able to bring wars and conquests to an end, what was the world supposed to do in the 1900s? Especially given that wars in an industrial age were no longer fought on the back of horses with a bunch of metal armour featuring swords, shields, bows and arrows. Nor were wars solely fought on battlefields so to speak. Modern industrialised weaponry meant that the entire nature of war would be changed. Besides having navies to fight at sea and armies to fight on land, regimes now had to have an air force that would fight above the ground. This meant that regimes had the capacity to carpet bomb entire cities and wipe them out. And, many did exactly that.

In the early half of the 1900s, humanity had arrived at a unique junction never previously witnessed in world history. On the one hand, our ever-evolving world had delivered us a level of military technology that enabled regimes to cause unfathomable damage to their opponents during wars, through carpet bombings, aerial strikes and nukes. On the other hand, we had largely literate populations with basic education and mass media reporting on the details of government decisions. By comparison, the average peasant couldn't read nor write in the Middle Ages and there was no such thing as mass media. If a Monarch or a Pope commissioned a war, generally the gruesome scenes of dead bodies would be seen on the battlefield, away from the fortified walls of cities or villages where most of the civilian population lived. Except in the rare instance when cities and villages too were plundered, which they sometimes were, but that wasn't always the norm. So regular folks had no reason to develop an intense aversion towards war. If anything, they continued to think of wars and conquering (or 'stealing') new lands as the highest form of achievement, and the warriors who helped achieve new lands were thought of as heroes in almost the same way as we, modern folks, revere our sports celebrities.

This was no longer the case in the early 1900s. With wars being far more destructive and mass media making sure the average educated member of the population read about it in the newspaper and heard about it on the radio, perpetual war for war's sake, with endless desire to conquer and expand territories, could no longer afford to be the default *modus operandi* for ruling regimes. In large part, this is the reason that led to the rise of nationalism in the first place which worked hand in hand with waves of decolonisation. Wherever there were governments in place that ruled over a group of people who felt the government didn't represent their economic interests, or didn't represent the cultural, ethnic, linguistic, sectarian or religious identities of the majority of the local population, they took up arms to subvert such regimes and appoint ones that closely resembled local preferences. This backdrop carried within itself all the requisite conditions to facilitate an end to the old world order, where anyone who could raise an army and go conquering lands just did so and got away with it.

There needed to be a whole new effort that would achieve for the world what couldn't be achieved at Westphalia in 1648 and Vienna in 1815. So the next big development in humanity's quest to put an end to wars and conquests came in 1920 with the establishment of the League of Nations.[55] This body was largely seen as ineffective unless there was consensus among the powerful nations to in fact put an end to war by choice and to pursue the path of diplomacy to resolve their differences. Even though US President Woodrow Wilson had played a key role in establishing the League of Nations, he wasn't able to convince his own country, the United States, the emerging superpower to join the League.[56]

Having won the Spanish-American War of 1898 which gave the United States some key strategic outposts in the Asia-Pacific — not to mention its role in putting an end to World War I in 1918 — the United States had already established itself the reputation it continues to have to date that is, as a chief negotiator of peace and stability between nations. So if the US wasn't going to be a part of an inter-governmental body like the League of Nations, the prospects of global peace weren't going to last long, or so it was feared. After all, who was to help enforce the principle where there was a violation? Yet the reason why President Wilson couldn't get his own country to join the League was due to the prevalence of isolationist sentiment within the US Congress.

Earlier in 1823, another US President James Monroe had issued what has come to be known as the 'Monroe Doctrine', which basically argued that the two Americas would no longer be open to further exploration and colonisation by any European power.[57] This rather assertive decree essentially established the continents of North and South America as the US sphere of influence. It was often said that the Monroe Doctrine ought to be read inversely, that so long as foreign powers didn't intervene in American affairs inside its sphere, the US would also not intervene in the affairs of other countries. Each was to mind their own businesses, so to speak. Fast forward to 1920, the influence of this Monroe Doctrine was visible among large sections of the US Congress and the general public. Their view was that the United States would be better off minding its own business and not getting involved in global fights.

Now the big question was: What next? Was the League (1920) going to be cast into the archives of history as another flop like Westphalia (1648) and Vienna (1815)? In short, no. Little had anybody known, what came next was to be the turning point. Eight years later, a new pact was signed by the United States Secretary of State Frank B. Kellogg and the French Foreign Minister Aristide Briand. Its official title was *General Treaty for Renunciation of War as an Instrument of National Policy* – commonly referred to as the Kellogg-Briand Pact (1928).[58] This pact had 31 signatory nations, including the majority of those European powers that had set up colonies overseas. Like the previous two attempts at Westphalia and Vienna centuries earlier, the aim of this pact, as suggested in its title, was to renounce war. It was feared that humanity had, by this point of our social and technological evolution, reached a stage where continued wars involving modern industrialised weapons could potentially destroy planet earth and mark the end of humanity. Ironically though, as coming decades would show, this Kellogg-Briand Pact also struggled to put an end to war. But what it did do was that it put the thought of wars needing to be renounced in the minds of world leaders.

Unlike the case with the League of Nations (1920) eight years earlier, this time with the Kellogg-Briand Pact (1928) the United States didn't just start the concept, it actually came on board itself. This would be a major turning point for the world. Any organisation aiming to act like a quasi-world government with an intention to set down rules for the interaction between nation-states would require an enforcement mechanism. Rules are good for nothing without the ability to enforce. This is why we don't just have speed signs on the road in our jurisdictions on a voluntary compliance basis. We have no choice. We have to drive within the speed limit or we get penalised, it's that simple. How would a quasi-world government that is trying to outlaw territorial conquests penalise an offending regime or nation-state? This is precisely why the United States' involvement was so pivotal. It was and still remains the only country with both the military capability and the political will to be able to police another nation for an actual or perceived violation of the rules-based world order.

It was precisely due to the widespread coverage that this pact received, along with US involvement, that world leaders finally began to realise they couldn't just keep going as rulers had done for nearly 5,000 years of civilisation, that is, by going around conquering land and centralising access to natural resources forever. There was an overall raising of consciousness. So while World War II (1939-1945) still happened despite the Kellogg-Briand Pact, its aftermath carried all the requisite conditions for the world to come together and finally 'codify' this prohibition on land conquests. Recall the point that by this stage of history, weapons had become more destructive and literate populations had the capacity to follow the news and learn about the inherently destructive nature of war. World War II resulted in millions of civilian casualties and much of this was caught on video footage. Never before had the general public witnessed mass carnage of this nature that could only reinforce the appetite to outlaw expansionist war for its own sake.

The next logical step was the birth of the United Nations in 1945, right at the end of World War II. The UN essentially came to replace the League of Nations. Yet again, the idea wasn't entirely dissimilar from what had happened earlier at Westphalia (1648) or Vienna (1815) or the League (1920). The objective of this new inter-governmental organisation was, in fact, to keep world peace and ensure that diplomacy becomes the tool for negotiation and dispute resolution between nation-states rather than war. With this vision in mind, the United Nations adopted its Charter which contained several rules for how countries with UN membership were to behave as responsible members of an international community and work towards the overall betterment of humanity. Outlawing war was a major and necessary first step towards this goal. Article 2(4) of the UN Charter went on to prohibit the use of force against the territorial integrity of any sovereign state which effectively nullifies the Right of Conquest.[59] From that point on, the borders between countries were deemed fixed. Member nation-states were to honour each other's sovereignties. Independent states had to emerge on the basis of global consensus and recognition.

As much as this started to seem like a moment when humanity had finally got a grip on its primordial warring instincts, there was an arising question that couldn't be left unanswered. So if future conquests or territorial acquisitions by the use of force (future 'land thefts' as critics might say) were to be prohibited by the new UN Charter, where does that leave us as far as previous conquests or territorial acquisitions were concerned? This could be answered in one of two binary ways. Either, the law only applies prospectively (ie. to future conquests), which would've meant that aspiring countries could complain and argue that it's unfair how Portugal, Spain, France and England among others got to acquire so much land, monopolise access to so many natural resources, became the richest and most powerful nation-states on earth as a result, as well as got to export their cultures, beliefs, legal systems and languages to their colonial subjects, why can't others have the chance to do the same? This is where the conversation on colonialism turns tricky. There are no easy answers, but it's important to appreciate the complexity around this.

The minute one agrees that all this past colonialism was of tremendous economic advantage and value to the imperial power that got the chance to participate in it, a current aspiring regime would say it wants the same. If we let that happen, it's back to that old world order of perpetual warfare. Or, the other option was that the law applies retroactively as well, which would've meant that all previous conquests had to either be undone and completely decolonised, or reparations had to be paid to compensate for those 'land thefts'. Decolonisation is a lesser headache to implement where we're dealing with a non-settler colony, such as the Subcontinent. The vast majority of the inhabitants were of local stock with a small number of British settlers, mostly from the ruling or entrepreneurial classes there to govern or invest. Decolonisation meant a transfer of power to local representatives and leaving. But in settler colonies, such as Australia or New Zealand, where the colonising power had transferred its own British-born settlers to live and procreate in the conquered land alongside local populations, decolonisation isn't as simple as that. Human identities are constantly transforming and descendants of British settlers born in Australia or New Zealand would develop their own attachment to the land on which they currently live, not the land from which their ancestors came. Telling an Australian born person of British ancestry to 'go back to Britain' as part of a decolonisation mission would be utterly impractical.

In working through the logistics of the implementation of the UN Charter and the ban on future conquests, these are examples of the sorts of challenging questions that its architects would've had to encounter, knowing fully well there were no easy answers. The vast majority of this planet is a product of colonialism, imperialism and territorial expansion one way or another. Recall our point earlier about early Islamic conquests from the outskirts of Arabia right up to Spain in the west and China in the east. So if one were to go down this idealistic path of full scale decolonisation, does that only apply to the British Empire, or does it also apply to other conquests? If they apply to both, how does one decolonise a country like Egypt where Islam is now the default religion and Arabic is the mother tongue? In short, we can't, nor should we have to. One argument would be that Egypt has as much right to preserve its religiously Islamic and linguistically Arabic identity as colonised nations of the Anglosphere do, to preserve theirs.

Critics often argue that if early Islamic conquests are acceptable, then so should the conquests of the British Empire be acceptable. The whole of North and South America currently has countries on it that speak a mixture of Spanish, English and Portuguese. Countries like Mexico (a product of the Spanish Empire) and Brazil (a product of the Portuguese Empire) could be decolonised insofar as that meant independence from Spanish and Portuguese rule, with locally elected leaders running the show, a bit like what Australia went through upon becoming a Federation in 1901. In fact, this is precisely the form decolonisation did take in Mexico when it separated from the Spanish Empire in 1821 and in Brazil a year later when it too separated from the Portuguese Empire in 1822.

This was a form of decolonisation but not the kind some critics often expect, which involves more than just local political autonomy. That kind of a concept involves any cultural or linguistic remnants of the original conqueror's identity being removed from sight because it might offend Indigenous sensitivities. After centuries of cross-cultural exchange, the reality is that the idea of a Mexican and a Brazilian are by their very nature cultural and linguistic hybrids. In that, neither is a Mexican identical to a Spaniard, nor a Brazilian identical to Portuguese. Both national identities and their consciousnesses have picked up many native elements from earlier native American cultures to form a hybrid identity. Decolonising those is impossible. It's not just a matter of sending a few foreign rulers back to their countries of origin. The same is the case where conquered lands have produced a demographic majority of descendants of former colonisers. It's impossible to imagine the thought of deporting millions of descendants of the colonising class.

In realising these challenges, it was understood that the UN Charter wouldn't be imposed retroactively. In member countries, where there were organic cases of nationalist independence movements and decolonisation was practically achievable (for instance, the cases of India and Pakistan), the international community was to support the right of local populations to have self-determination. In the cases of countries where decolonisation was impractical due to the formation of cross-cultural hybrid identities (meaning the coloniser and the colonised) being submerged into each other (for instance, Mexico and Brazil), then past conquests would simply be deemed to be legitimate gains. Now the question arose, how does one determine where to set the statute of limitations for what was to be considered legitimate territorial gains? The answer ended up drawing on the Kellogg-Briand Pact (1928) and set the year of the signing of this pact as the cut-off for determining what was to be deemed 'legitimate' conquests. Although the UN Charter does not make any direct references to this pact, it sort of came to be an unofficial deadline. In other words, if a piece of land was acquired through exploration, discovery, settlement, conquest or colonisation *before* 1928, that was generally deemed lawful. This little known but significant theme has been explored at length in Oona Hathaway and Scott Shapiro's joint book *The Internationalists: And Their Plan to Outlaw War* (2017).[60] With 1928 acting as the cut-off for legitimate conquests, no decolonisation was expected, unless there was a compelling case and it was practical to do so. Since the enactment of the UN Charter in 1945, this has been the chief convention regulating territorial acquisitions as part of the United States-led, rules-based world order.

While both wars and border changes have continued to take place since the adoption of the intentions of the Kellogg-Briand Pact (1928) since the UN Charter was issued in 1945, the point to note is that war is no longer thought of as an instrument of diplomacy. By contrast, under the old world order, let's say you had a dispute with another country, you'd simply launch an all-out invasion instead of negotiating as a measure of first resort. There is more awareness around this now. The United States has participated in more wars than most countries since the UN Charter and to a large extent, the reason is because the United States takes upon itself the responsibility to be the global police. Recall our earlier point that the League of Nations (1920) was bound to be unsuccessful due to its inability to enforce rules due to isolationists in the US preventing their country from joining. The League effectively became a defunct institution as a result and was eventually substituted by the United Nations, with full support from the United States. There is an International Court of Justice (ICJ) where disputes between nations are dealt with and an International Criminal Court (ICC) where rogue leaders are supposed to be trialled.[61] Although, if there is an unwarranted armed conflict somewhere in the world, it's impossible for there not to be a military response to stop the war. If the war isn't stopped through a counter-offensive, then the question of charging anyone is out of the equation. This makes the enforcement of international law a real challenge.

It's with a vision to address this challenge and to help maintain global stability that the United States has over time built more than 800 military bases around the world across every continent.[62] This is a contentious issue which remains the subject of widespread debate and criticism. Many argue that these military bases give the United States undue ability to meddle in any other country's affairs and use it to advance its strategic interests. This theme has been explored at length in David Vine's *The United States of War: A Global History of America's Endless Conflicts, from Columbus to the Islamic State* (2021).[63] This is a fascinating topic in its own right, but delving into it isn't entirely relevant to the purpose of this book. The United States has always insisted that it has taken it upon itself to help the United Nations enforce rules to maintain global stability. As the United States has found itself involved in wars even after the UN Charter across Korea (1950-1953), Vietnam (1955-1975), Afghanistan (2001-2021) and Iraq (2003-2011) to use four notable examples, it has to date insisted that it didn't invade and occupy these countries for imperialism nor hegemony.

Rather, the United States has long insisted that the role it played in these wars was that of a peacemaker. It was either there fighting communism because that's apparently an evil ideology that had to be stopped at all cost, or it was there to liberate oppressed people from what it saw at the time as tyrannical dictatorship with weapons of mass destruction.

It's important to bear these points in mind, otherwise we could be confused and end up dismissing the UN Charter altogether on the basis that since its biggest supporter the United States itself breaks the rules so often, why should other countries be held to a different standard? What's equally important to touch on are territorial acquisitions by use of force that have *continued* to take place *despite* the UN Charter prohibiting this practice and making future conquests unlawful. Unless this topic is addressed in advance, a critic might pick up on the fact that borders have continued to be redrawn despite the UN Charter and start questioning if the gap between the old and the new world orders isn't so wide after all.

It's true, there have been instances where borders have continued to change due to war despite the UN Charter as the case used to be in the old world. Why is that the case? Let's take a closer look at those cases. The most notable case was that of India's annexation of Goa in 1961.[64] Goa was conquered by the Portuguese Empire in 1510 and had remained under its control ever since. India's claim was that in the past Goa had been part of India and most of the inhabitants who lived there were of Indian ancestry and while the rest of India had been decolonised from the British Empire, this little town shouldn't be left under colonial occupation. India got away with its irredentist claims because there was widespread public support for the move among the Goanese people. They were all given Indian citizenship and that was the end of that issue. Nobody dares to claim that Goa is under Indian 'occupation'.

The other case is that of Turkey's invasion of northern Cyprus in 1974.[65] This has been widely condemned but again, Turkey has a similar justification. It argues that since northern Cyprus is made up of ethnic Turks who would be disadvantaged under an ethnic Greek majority Cyprus, it makes sense for Turkey to be the one to rule the ethnically Turkish parts of Cyprus. This remains the subject of widespread debate, but Turkey has, by and large, taken this land without serious pushback from the international community. It continues to remain a part of powerful global institutions such as NATO and the UN itself. The final case is the most complicated of all to address, that is Israel's control over the lands it captured in 1967 from its Arab neighbours. Israel took the Golan Heights from Syria, the Sinai Peninsula and the Gaza Strip from Egypt and the West Bank from Jordan. Israel ended up giving the Sinai Peninsula back to Egypt in gradual stages upon the signing of a peace treaty between 1979 and 1982. Israel withdrew from the Gaza Strip in 2005 but continued to put the region under a blockade for what it insists are security concerns. Israel re-invaded Gaza in late 2023 following a surprise attack by Hamas along the southern border.[66] The Israel-Gaza war was still on-going at the time of writing this book. Back to the territorial gains from 1967, Israel annexed the Golan Heights in 1981 citing security concerns that may arise if the region was to ever be handed back to Syria. Israel has offered a pathway to achieving Israeli citizenship to the local ethno-religious Druze villagers that reside in the region.

What's left is the status of the West Bank which remains unresolved. While Israel controls the borders, the airspace and critical infrastructure within the West Bank, it hasn't formally annexed this piece of land as a whole. The only part of the West Bank that has been annexed is East Jerusalem in 1980 due to its centrality to Jewish tradition. Israel can't just officially annex the West Bank because it is presently (or was, at the time of writing this book), home to 3 million Palestinian Arabs and absorbing them all as Israeli citizens would create a demographic imbalance that would undermine the Jewish demographic majority which the State of Israel in its pre-1967 borders presently enjoys with 7 million Jewish and 2 million Arab citizens. Absorbing another 3 million, if the West Bank were to be annexed at this time, would mean 5 million Arab and 7 million Jewish citizens. Israel has continued to transfer its Jewish citizens into the West Bank with an intention to achieve a demographic majority on that piece of land. The West Bank remains divided into three zones. Area A is under limited Palestinian control. Area B is under joint Palestinian-Israeli control. Area C is under full Israeli control and some 500,000 Jewish residents have been transferred into this area in recent decades. The fact that 2 million Palestinian Arabs in Gaza have had to remain under a blockade and another 3 million across Areas A and B of the West Bank remain under limited autonomy with neither full citizenship nor an independent state of their own makes this topic more complex to discuss than almost any other in geopolitics. Israel's response to most criticism directed towards itself is by citing security concerns and ancient Jewish historic connection to the land.

There have been instances where countries have launched full scale invasions of other countries and not gotten away with it. Saddam Hussein tried to capture Kuwait in August 1990 and was driven out by the United States and its allies by February 1991. Vladimir Putin invaded Ukraine in February 2022. Many experts suggested NATO enlargement[67] and Ukrainian marginalisation of ethnic Russians in Ukraine's eastern region were the contributing factors.[68] Because Russia is a superpower equipped with nuclear weapons and a major exporter of oil, gas and coal, no country has stepped in to defend Ukraine directly, as they did with Kuwait. There is widespread condemnation directed towards Russia as a result of President Vladimir Putin's decision to launch its military operation in Ukraine. The situation was unresolved at the time of writing this book.

As we can see, while this little known Kellogg-Briand Pact struggled to enforce its noble objectives at the time of its signing in 1928, the aftermath of World War II in 1945 saw it end up forming the basis for the prohibition on future conquests after the adoption of the United Nations Charter the same year.[69] After previous unsuccessful attempts by the Treaty of Westphalia (1648), the Congress of Vienna (1815) and the League of Nations (1920), humanity had finally evolved to the point where no nation-state, under this revised world order, was to acquire or annex new territories by the use of force, or what was once known as the Right of Conquest. In doing so, it was ensured the law wouldn't be applied retroactively because that would result in an endless series of irredentist claims seeking territorial re-adjustments across almost every country, depending on how far back we anchor in our starting point. That would've thrown the entire world map into disarray because, humans being migratory species by both the creationist and evolutionist accounts as discussed earlier, have always moved around from place to place. Virtually every country has, at some point, been home to another human community one doesn't consider to be its own. Having 1928 as the cut-off for determining the legitimacy of territorial conquests would preserve the integrity of international borders.

Now that we have thoroughly discussed the nature and evolution of international conventions and laws around conquests, as well as the issues arising out of those, recall that we discussed earlier how the concept of a 'stolen land' could either be a statement from legality or it could be a statement from morality. As far as legality is concerned, Australia was claimed for the British Crown by Captain James Cook in 1770 and its settlement began as a settler penal colony from 1788 onwards. Australia has a demographic majority of descendants of British ancestors. Australia's discovery and settlement began 140 years before that cut-off of 1928. Everyone in Australia, regardless of ethnic or religious backgrounds, is entitled to citizenship and full Parliamentary representation, which negates the need for an organic decolonisation movement. In light of each of these facts and the conventions of international law, Australia is not illegally built on 'stolen land'. It is a legitimate country like many others, with a legitimate and inclusive national identity. Those descendants of earlier generations of British settlers not only make up the majority of our population, they're also the ones mainly responsible for building this country up into being what it has become – a liberal, democratic country where aspiring individuals are provided equal opportunity to chase their dreams more so than in most societies. This explains why millions of folks from all over the world have chosen to call Australia home. Remember that people don't choose to settle in inherently 'racist' countries built on 'stolen land'. It would be counter-intuitive if they did.

The only angle now left to cover is a moral one. It is entirely possible that, even after reading this fairly thorough discussion, some critics still say that just because something is *legal* doesn't make it *moral*. As a matter of principle, that's obviously true – it doesn't. We acknowledged earlier that, even in an anarchic state of play, there are certain things that would still be wrong. If a consciously owned object was stolen from its owner and if the owner was known, then taking the object away would be morally wrong even if the entire jurisdiction, written laws and courts had collapsed. This requires us to mount a separate case for why Australia is not built on stolen land from a moral standpoint. There are several issues at play here. At the time when Captain Cook arrived here in 1770, his instructions were to take possession of the land with the consent of the natives. Often critics make the British Empire out to be one which was inherently racist and dismissive towards native populations over the course of Australia's settlement, but this was not the case on the overwhelming majority of occasions. One example is the issuing of Letters Patent establishing the Province of South Australia in 1836. In these Letters, the British authorities specified the recognition of the rights of Indigenous peoples inhabiting South Australia at the time.

This was not the act of a dismissive or oppressive regime, but rather an early attempt at codifying Indigenous rights and liberties within English-made law. Additionally, the types of British people who used to enlist to become privateers, explorers and sea merchants were usually quite curious about other cultures and appreciated dealing with different kinds of people. Captain Cook was no exception. He, in fact, had many fond things to say in his journal entries about the native populations he came into contact with. One example was his description of Indigenous people along the coast of New South Wales. Cook wrote: 'There [sic.] features are far from being disagreeable, and their Voices are soft and Tunable' and 'I do not look upon them to be a warlike people; on the contrary, I think them a Timorous and inoffensive race, no ways inclined to Cruelty, as appear'd from their behaviour to one of our people in Endeavour River'.[70]

Next door to Australia, the same British Empire had gone on to sign the Treaty of Waitangi in 1840 with a coalition of Maori tribal elders. This harmonious way of acquiring and settling new lands for the Crown is attributable to the British Empire's relatively humane temperament in comparison to the Spanish conquistadors discussed earlier. The Spaniards had shown little mercy to the natives in the Americas. The question arises: Why would the British not opt to sign a treaty in Australia, when they signed one in New Zealand next door? In short, because there was no one group to sign a treaty with. Neither did the island continent of Australia have a central authority or some form of representative government that could speak for most native inhabitants, nor did the vast majority of Indigenous tribes have any concept of private property ownership the way the concept was understood in Europe. The Maoris of New Zealand did have tribal chiefs with whom the Brits could negotiate. In Australia's case, it was not possible to 'steal' that which was neither owned by a representative government, nor for the most part owned by private owners.

The size of mainland Australia is 7.688 million km^2 which is more than a dozen times larger than the size of an average country by today's standards. The vast majority of mainland Australia was even less inhabitable back then, than it is today. Many inland areas have been terraformed through deliberate town planning made conducive to human survival by British settlement. Yet despite these efforts, more than 95% of Australia's population lives in close proximity to the coastal areas of the country. As can be seen from this map.

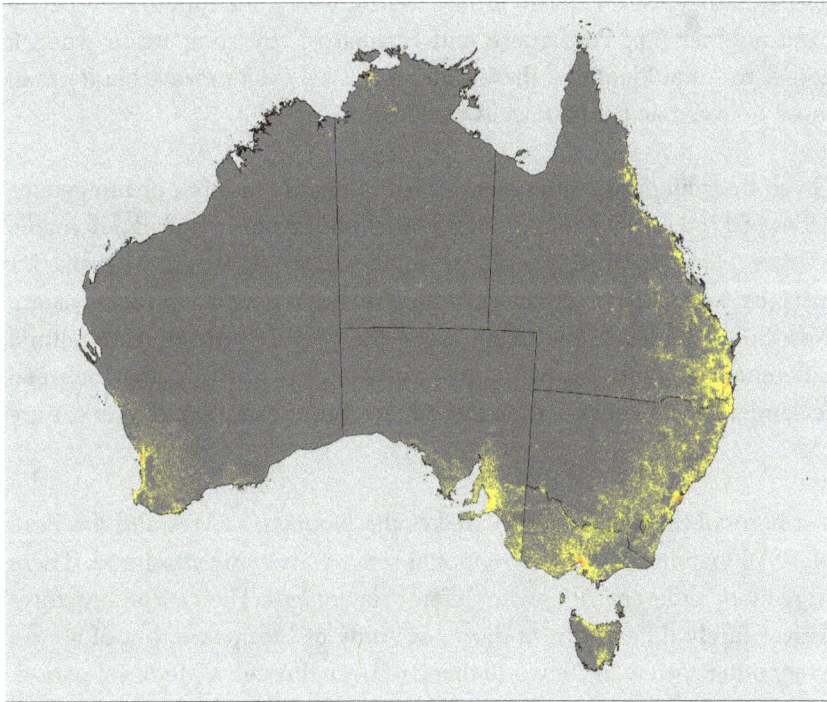

(Source: Wikimedia Commons)

When British settlement began in 1788, the total Indigenous population is estimated to be around 750,000.[71] Their exact dispersion across the island continent is difficult to assess, despite the fact that present-day activists have produced maps showing more than 250 different 'nations' that lived on this island.[72] It is indisputable that there were diverse groups of Indigenous tribes present on the island, though classifying them as 'nations' in the conventional sense might be well-intentioned, it is still misleading. There is no shortage of tribal societies in the world. Tribes exist in many Arabic-speaking countries, most notably in Saudi Arabia. Many of the Bedouin communities who reside in the deserts of the Arabian Peninsula today live a nomadic lifestyle not entirely dissimilar from that of Indigenous Australians before 1788. Each tribe has a way of distinguishing itself from another tribe, often based on differences that would inevitably seem trivial to the outside observer. Even national identities, which are supposed to be the more organised of the two constructs seem trivial at times when we start weighing up differences and similarities between two groups to justify why one should be separate from another (i.e. Portuguese and Spaniards), by comparison when it comes to tribal identities, these differences are even more arbitrary than those between actual nations as we know them.

Given their linguistic differences, it is reasonable to think of Indigenous tribes in 1788 as belonging to different ethnic groups who led a nomadic lifestyle. The Noongar people of south-western Western Australia for instance had little in common with the Eora people of south-eastern New South Wales. Some might argue the ethnic, linguistic and cultural difference between the two could be nearly as much as that between Icelanders and Greeks — though both are Europeans, the differences are vast.

Yet none of this automatically makes the Noongar of WA and the Eora of NSW 'nations' in the conventional sense warranting statehood. There were many different tribes with different languages. Their social structures were entirely different from those, not only of Europeans, but of almost every other society in the world that had been through a Medieval period. As most tribes were nomadic people who wandered from place to place and did not have a central government, it is unreasonable to suggest that every single square cm of the entire 7.688 million km^2 of the island continent should have been left alone by anyone who didn't identify as an Indigenous Australian. We have touched on the point about humans being a migratory species with great regularity throughout this chapter.

All lands have been settled and re-settled by multiple groups of people. Britain itself has been invaded countless times, by Romans in 55 BCE, by German tribes in 410, by the Vikings in 793, by the Normans in 1066 and by the Danish in 1069 to name a few. England had a lot less land than the giant island continent of Australia to share with everyone who crossed the English Channel. Yet through the wear and tear of history, England managed to adapt and survive — as did many other nations. In an age without the Kellogg-Briand Pact or the UN Charter, of course it was natural and inevitable that lands would be conquered and re-conquered, be that England's own case a thousand years earlier, or that of Australia in 1770 when Captain Cook claimed it. This was a giant and under-utilised island that was sparsely populated.

To sum up, Australia in 1788 had no central, Indigenous structure or representative government. Most of it was uninhabited. The areas that were inhabited were sparsely populated. Its inhabitants had a concept of property ownership vastly different from that understood by the British at the time. It had lots of vacant land along the inhabitable coastal areas close to the sources of water. Britain didn't colonise with malicious intentions. It did so out of necessity in search of a new penal colony, having lost America. It did so with the express aim of showing respect and courtesy towards the natives as instructed by the Crown. In fact, where there was an identifiable tribal chiefdom, the British settlers evidently did negotiate treaties, such as in New Zealand's case. In claiming and settling Australia, the British Empire acted in accordance with the global conventions and norms of the pre-United Nations world order. The British Empire was far from perfect, but it was committed to subjecting itself to some higher principles, some might argue ahead of its time. Earlier on, we established that Australia isn't stolen land from a legal standpoint. Now, we have established that Australia isn't stolen land from a moral standpoint either. We should all continue to care for and empathise with our fellow Indigenous Australians. We should all commit to doing our bit to improve the lives of all Australians which by definition includes both Indigenous and non-Indigenous Australians. We shouldn't have to look down on other cultures, and especially not Indigenous culture since its contributions to our national story are rich and worthy of admiration. That said, we must not allow the cause for Indigenous empowerment to be hijacked by a small number of vocal activists with a misguided view of our country as a nation built on 'stolen land'.

5

Does Australia have a way of life?

Australia's critics often question whether the country even has a distinct enough culture or way of life. As we've seen in other defining features of Australian political debate, these are usually one-sided statements posed as rational queries. By asking whether Australia has a way of life, what critics are implying is that in *their* view it doesn't. Some modern media pundits like to think of Australia as devoid of any defining cultural values or way of life. The editorial board of Victorian newspaper, *The Age*, even went so far as to publish an article entitled *Oi: no such thing as Australian values* in June 2018.[73] The editors cautioned the public that: 'a nationalist filter should not be allowed to undermine and distract from universal human values.' The use of throwaway phrases such as 'universal human values' runs the risk of railroading any discussion of Australian identity into a meaningless and empty pit where what it means to be distinctly Australian becomes conflated with the idea of a 'global village'. If the High Court of Australia found the early British settlers were wrong in their description of our country as *terra nullius,* then the modern critics are wrong in their description of it as a *cultura nullius.*

This issue also needs to be taken seriously because it too carries a greater concern for Australia's future than we may consciously realise. Think about it, if Australia doesn't even have its own culture, then it makes eminent sense to support open borders as public policy. The justification would be that cultural diversity imported from foreign nations only helps enrich our society by filling our 'cultureless' void. If, on the other hand, it was established that Australia does have a distinct way of life worth preserving, that then shifts the whole debate. This chapter examines this criticism and argues that Australia *does* in fact have a way of life based on an improved version of British culture and the embrace of cultural diversity for its own sake does undermine our capacity to ensure national self-preservation.

As a starting point, even those who allege that Australia doesn't have a culture ironically don't tend to say the same about Britain, the parent country. On a superficial level, they might be prepared to accept that everything from William Shakespeare to Mr Bean to the changing of guards at Buckingham Palace to Bangers & Mash to a cold ale at a cosy pub to watching Manchester United at Old Trafford to test cricket at Lord's to political rallies at Hyde Park to a symphony orchestra at the Royal Albert Hall are all valid representations of the British way of life. If it's established that Britain has an identifiable culture, how is it then that its colonial off-shoot Australia supposedly doesn't? The thought makes little sense. It almost implies that British settlers got to Australia then somehow *lost* track of their culture − what a weird thought. Australia's culture is essentially an improved version of working class British culture from the mid-1800s. Exceptions aside, cultures don't usually remain fixed in particular forms forever. They tend to evolve over time. Cultures tend to adapt to the realities and social pressures of the timeframes in which they exist, but usually continue to survive as part of a continuum.

To understand where Australia's culture and way of life come from, we have to take a couple of steps back and reflect on their points of origin − working class British culture at the time of settlement. Like most societies at the time, Britain too had a rigid class structure. This sounds off-putting to the modern ear for entirely understandable reasons. But it's worth noting that back then, other cultures and societies were hardly any different. China, for centuries, had had distinct social classes: The Shi were scholars and officials. The Nong were peasants and farmers. The Gong were artisans. The Shang were merchants. The Chinese Emperor sat atop the lot of them. Right at the bottom were the slaves.[74] India had a similar social structure: The Brahmins were the priests. The Kshatria were the warriors. The Vaishyas were merchants and landowners. The Shudras were commoners, peasants and servants. The last of these are often referred to as the 'untouchables'.[75] England in the late 1700s was pretty similar. It had a social structure not entirely dissimilar from the Chinese and Indian cases, without the same naming conventions. The ruling elite, also called the aristocracy, ran the country. There was barely any opportunity for upward social mobility.

Whatever class or social status you happened to be born in, falling short of a stroke of luck, you would more or less be stuck within that class for the rest of your life. Being part of the aristocracy meant a life of privilege — top education, top nutrition, top networks right across the entire social and political architecture of English society. Nepotism and cronyism were rampant across all sectors. People who were well-connected in that rigid social hierarchy could get around the system for personal benefit. By contrast, those at the bottom were too often left optionless in the face of adversity. The press wasn't quite free to publish proper criticism of the government. In the rare instance when critics did voice their views, the consequences could be severe. Women were treated as subordinate. Poverty was so rife that small thefts were commonplace. People often stole apples, bananas or a loaf of bread just to survive. This explains why British prisons were also over-crowded. The British aristocracy was, by and large, perceived by the commoner as a bunch of snobs. Their mannerisms and general demeanour were often considered to be overly dismissive and judgemental towards those of a lower social status.

This is the cultural backdrop against which Australia was founded. As a newborn society, while Australia did inherit the language, customs and the legal and political systems from its parent country, it threw the rigid aspects of Britain's society out the window. This has been the defining essence of the Australian way of life ever since — even though it's rare for Australia to be thought of in those terms. Many of the discriminatory customs of English society were either immediately or eventually purged from the emerging cultural fabric of Australian society. The earliest example of this comes in the very year of our founding. There were two convicts named Henry Kable and Susannah Holmes on board the ship HMS Alexander in 1788 on their way to Australia as part of the First Fleet. They were convicted thieves who had met at Norwich Castle Jail not long before being deported to the upcoming penal colony that was to be New South Wales. The pair had originally been sentenced to capital punishment, but got lucky enough to end up on the First Fleet instead.

Soon after arriving in Australia, the couple realised their luggage had gone missing. Now note that in England at the time, convicts were routinely denied the right to hold property or bring on legal proceedings. This couple went ahead and sought an explanation about their missing items. Captain Duncan Sinclair of HMS Alexander was brought before the Court. Unable to provide a satisfactory explanation about the missing luggage, he was ordered to pay the couple £15 in compensation for their loss.[76] Justice was served — even for a notorious convict couple. Henry eventually went on to become a successful businessman and the chief constable of the colony of New South Wales. What is fascinating is that the proceeding took place in the English language, under Common Law, and the compensation was awarded in English currency – all of which are inheritances from the parent country, yet the fact that the case concerned two individuals who never would've been able to stand in court seeking justice due to being convicts back in England is what makes Australia different.

Remember that every society and nation is a product of its past, Australia is no exception. What the story of Henry Kable and Susannah Holmes tells us is the principle that all Australians were to live under the rule of law — laying down the foundations for what would be a society with equality before the law. Just because you were of a lower socio-economic status, this did not mean that you should be denied basic legal rights. Yet this little known story is only the beginning. The period from settlement in 1788 to Federation in 1901 represents Australia's formative years. It's when this society got to work out what its identity would be and how its values would shape up. This happened through a mixture of serendipity and deliberate effort on the part of certain individuals. In addition to equality, we as modern-day Australians are accustomed to hearing about the freedoms of thought, speech and press. We like to think that in this place, we're free to think what we want, to say what we think and to publish it to wider audiences without the fear of censorship or persecution. This has become one of the central tenets of our way of life. But these freedoms also weren't handed on a plate.

Another English convict, by the name of Andrew Bent, was transported to Hobart in 1812 following his conviction for burglary. Australia in those days had inherited the same laws as England for regulating what its press could publish. The authorities of the day were naturally anxious about the direction that public opinion might end up taking. These anxieties were reinforced by the growing number of revolts and revolutions against the governments of the day incited within various societies across Europe and America. In 1816, Bent started running his newspaper the *Hobart Town Gazette*. An on-going challenge was that a government-appointed editor had the final say over what could and couldn't be printed. Over coming years, Bent became increasingly frustrated by the fact that Lieutenant Governor George Arthur of Van Diemen's Land (now, Tasmania) was censoring the content and with that, limiting his and every other critic's ability to offer constructive criticism on crucial public policy matters. In 1824, Bent decided to print edition 422 of the *Gazette* without sending the government appointed Editor Henry Emmett the draft before publishing.

Bent was later charged £518 and sentenced to six months in prison. He ended up losing his printing contracts, but continued to publish anyway. He was prosecuted for libel in 1828, 1830 and 1836. On these occasions, he was only fined but not imprisoned. Bent and his family left Tasmania in 1839 for Sydney where he started a weekly paper called *Bent's News* and *New South Wales Advertiser*.[77] His persistent efforts eventually earned him the permission to keep doing what he did best over the next few years, that was to publish his frank opinions on the politics of the day. This marked the beginning of the freedom of press in Australia. Bent was given the title 'The Tasmanian Franklin' after American revolutionary leader Benjamin Franklin. As we saw with the story of Henry and Susannah, equality wasn't an inherent feature of English society back then, but it would be so for Australian society. Likewise, Bent's triumph over media censorship rules established that governments weren't above criticism. That a free press was to be part and parcel of a vibrant democracy.

It's precisely stories like these that help us have clarity around who we are as a nation with its distinct culture and way of life, which is a product of past events like the ones we've just discussed — equality and freedom of press. Another feature of Australian culture is religious tolerance. This is yet another feature that didn't exist in the parent country the way it came to be in Australia. Since King Henry VIII's establishment of the Church of England (also known as the Anglican Church), sectarian divisions between Catholics and Protestants had been a regular feature of society across the British Isles. As religious persecution of Catholics became commonplace in mainland Britain, many escaped to neighbouring Ireland. When Australia began to be settled, its population demographics came from all over the British Isles. This meant that early Australia soon became a melting pot for English, Welsh, Scottish and Irish settlers along with their sectarian differences. The carryover of sectarian tensions on Australian soil was somewhat inevitable. A notable example of this is found in the Castle Hill Riot of 1804 – an unsuccessful attempt by Irish Catholic convicts to establish Irish rule. It also aimed to allow willing Catholic convicts to sail back to Ireland to participate in the on-going uprising that was already taking place.

It was in this situation that colonial authorities at the time sought to introduce measures to bring the simmering tensions to a calm. The defining feature of this effort was the *Church Act* (1836) introduced by the Irish-born Governor of New South Wales, Sir Richard Bourke. This piece of law laid down the provisions for government subsidies of clerical salaries, the construction of new churches and land grants for religious sites and schools on completely equal basis.[78] The non-discriminatory nature of this decision that deliberately overlooked sectarian differences within Christianity was remarkable for its time. Later, the Jewish faith also went on to be included in these provisions. This is yet another example of something uniquely Australian that happened here, which wouldn't have been quite so likely in England, that has since gone on to be a defining feature of Australian culture and way of life. Over time, Australia has continued to maintain and grow its commitment to pluralism and religious tolerance.

The year 1851 saw the discovery of gold in Victoria, a period otherwise known as the Gold Rush. There were a few of these across different regions where Europeans had set up remote colonies around the world. Many miners had flocked to Victoria in pursuit of employment. At the time, only property owning males had the right to vote. This counted most of the miners out. Yet they were expected to pay a fee to obtain a licence regardless of whether or not they ended up finding gold. This almost became another case of 'taxation without representation' as we had seen decades earlier inspiring the American revolution. Civil unrest erupted and following clashes between more than 10,000 gold diggers and the Victorian police, in the end the government responded by abolishing the mining licence fee altogether. 113 gold miners were arrested and 13 required to stand trial. Although public sentiment was so heavily in their favour that they all ended up being acquitted. The miners also ended up earning the right to be represented in parliament.[79] Known as the Eureka Stockade, this story has since gone on to become a defining moment in Australia's journey.[80] It established that Australia wouldn't be a society of government excess and one where everyone would be treated fairly. The whole concept of a 'fair go' being part of Australia's way of life can trace itself back to the Eureka Stockade.

Back in the day, even though Britain was running a democracy, it wasn't all smooth sailing. When it was time to vote, you had to scribble your choice on a piece of paper where everyone could see. They'd even yell out who you voted for. Since politicians weren't getting paid back then, it was mainly the rich blokes with plenty of land who could afford to be in politics. And if they found out you didn't vote for them, they weren't shy about causing you a few headaches. This was the dodgy system Australia picked up from the British in the early days. People started arguing about running our own show and making sure everyone could vote without any dramas. Then, in the mid-1800s, the British finally decided to let Victoria do its own thing with the Victorian Constitution Act. Bill Nicholson, who used to be the Mayor of Melbourne, chucked in a new law to let people vote without everyone knowing their business. Even though the rich and powerful weren't keen, the law got through at the start of 1856. That's how Victoria ended up being the first place in the world to let us vote in secret.[81]

Starting in Victoria, after Australia became the first place to kick off secret voting, the practice was later adopted by Tasmania and South Australia. The other states also caught on pretty quick after that. This way of voting in secret set the bar worldwide and even Britain and the United States picked it up later on. Every time we rock up to vote without anyone peeping at who we're ticking off on our ballots, we've got those early Australian pioneers to thank for making voting private. Who could argue that it's no one else's business to know who we're voting for, unless of course we choose to tell on our own. We don't wish to see people's personal choices exposed publicly, especially if they're at risk of being harassed. This commitment to privacy has since remained a central feature of the Australian way of life.

Despite the fact that Australia is often accused of being a racist country, as discussed in the previous chapter, the fact is that Australia showed signs to the contrary from its earliest days on. In a timeframe that's so widely presumed to be morbidly racist, we noted earlier that in 1868 an Australian cricket team, made up entirely of Indigenous Australians, travelled from Victoria to England as the first international sporting representatives from colonial Australia.[82] This team played 47 matches against various English teams winning 14, losing 14 and drawing 19. This Indigenous team was both literally and figuratively treated as equals to every other cricketer regardless of ancestral background. It was William Hayman who formed this team from members of three Indigenous tribes: Jardwadjali, Gunditjmara and Wotjobaluk. Only two years earlier, Captain and Coach Tom Wills and Hayman had organised a Boxing Day match against the Melbourne Cricket Club.

Although this all-Indigenous Australian team was defeated, the event attracted close to 8,000 spectators and inspired a tour of Victoria and New South Wales, and eventually England. Widely known for being Australia's first celebrity cricketer and the founder of Australian Rules Football, Wills was also well-regarded for his commitment to equality on the sporting field. His role in making the Indigenous Australian cricket tour of England happen is hardly surprising. His biographer Greg De Moore described Wills as "...a sportsman down to his bootlaces" who saw Indigenous Australians "...as equals in sport, something very few others at the time did. He saw a man as a sportsman, not by his face."[83] The fact that Australia has had a merit-based sporting culture that sees past race is too a defining feature of our way of life.

For most of world history, there had been a distinction between the roles of women and men. The patriarchal culture of the British Isles had been no different from the rest of the world at the time. Australia could've simply inherited this culture as it was — but it didn't. Instead, it led the charge in enfranchising women through the *Commonwealth Franchise Act* (1902) literally a year after we became a Federation. This piece of legislation was introduced by Senator Richard O'Connor in the upper house and MP William Lyne in the lower house. The Act granted women the right to vote in federal elections as well as be able to run for Parliament. Although the Colony of New Zealand had granted women the vote in 1893, it is worth noting out of interest that it wasn't a sovereign country at the time and wouldn't go on to become one until 1907. Australia's embrace of women's suffrage a year after its appearance on the world map as a federated nation-state makes it the first country to facilitate women's right to vote in elections.[84] By contrast, it took Britain itself decades to play catch up. It wasn't until 1928 that women had universal suffrage in UK elections. The *Commonwealth Franchise Act* (1902) was not only a major turning point in Australian history, but also in world history. At the individual level, gender discrimination exists across most societies and Australia is no exception. What matters in the end are the steps a society takes as a whole towards ensuring gender equality and mutual respect. Looking at what this little known act was able to achieve in 1902, there is little doubt that at the institutional level, treating women and men as political equals has been ingrained in Australian culture ever since.

The early settlers from Britain figured they had to learn to survive in the harsh Australian outback. This island continent was nothing like the green pastures of England or the Scottish highlands back home. As part of their efforts to adapt and survive, they developed a culture of mateship. This more or less meant that everyone had to do their bit to look after the rest without expecting to get something back in return. Not much makes for a better example of this than the birth of our surf life saving clubs across the nation. It's a little-known fact, in the mid-1800s, laws were in place prohibiting people from swimming at the beach during the day in Sydney. As attitudes towards public decency evolved, there was a significant increase in the number of beach goers. Being girt (as in, surrounded) by sea as our national anthem reminds us, it's hardly surprising that by the early 1900s, Australian coastal towns had developed a culture of swimming. We still have that in place.

More Australians going for a dip in the ocean meant more Australians at risk of drowning. Some sort of safety measures had to be put in place to save lives when needed. It was this vision in 1907 that led to the establishment of the Bondi Surf and Bathers' Life Saving Club by 23 volunteers. This was the first organisation of its kind at the time. The idea was that this would be a group of experienced divers and swimmers who would come together to volunteer their time at the beach. In case anyone was spotted drowning, they would jump out to rescue them. Volunteers from the Bondi Surf Club have saved an estimated 600,000 lives since the organisation was established.[85] It remains the world's oldest surf lifesaving club. The spirit of volunteerism has since been an integral feature of the Australian way of life. There are countries around the world where leaders often portray themselves as invincible. They put up what may seem to outsiders like a disproportionate number of posters of themselves on giant billboards. They are known for erecting huge statues of themselves at public squares. None of that stuff flies in Australia. People like former NSW Premier Mike Baird and 28th Prime Minister Tony Abbott were members of their local Queenscliff Surf Life Saving Club.[86] That embrace of the spirit of volunteerism earnt both of them plenty more respect in the eyes of the public than exaggerated billboards and statues do.

This nation of volunteers is built on a vast piece of land relative to its sparse population. The geographical isolation from major town centres in the early days meant that the country's inhabitants often lacked access to basic amenities, social services and medical facilities. Being aware of this challenge, in 1928 Reverend John Flynn established the Royal Flying Doctor Service with a vision to provide emergency medical treatment to Australians in remote locations, and to transport patients to the nearest hospital.[87] When Reverend Flynn first established this service, his goal was for it to act as an air ambulance and transport patients from remote areas to the nearest hospital. Almost a century later, the service not only exists, it has in fact saved thousands of lives over the years.

This 'air ambulance' continues to service more than 7 million Australians in remote and rural areas. It has since become one of the largest organisations for volunteering to serve the community. The Royal Flying Doctor Service has gone on to be seen as the gold standard for similar services to emerge in other countries. While the organisation has now come to receive government assistance in order to help meet the much higher demand for its services today, the fact remains that it was originally built entirely by volunteers and sustained through charity. This uniquely Australian community spirit stands as proof of our unity as one.

With all these little known stories that we have just run through in the present chapter, the point was not to draw these to your attention just because they sound cool. That's not even it. The question we're tackling here is whether or not we actually have a distinct culture or way of life in Australia, which is too often asked by those who doubt that we do. It's with an intention to respectfully respond to such critics that these little known stories are brought to your attention here. After all, stories are what defines our values, culture and way of life. Every society is a product of past events and we're no exception. If we take a close look at all the stories we have looked at in this chapter so far, we will realise each of them sums up a basic Australian value. We find equality in the Kable Case (1788), free press in Andrew Bent (1824), religious tolerance in the *Church Act* (1836), fair go for workers in the Eureka Stockade (1854), political privacy and freedom of association in the Secret Ballot (1856), racial equality in the Indigenous cricket team (1868), gender equality when it comes to voting in the *Commonwealth Franchise Act* (1902) and lastly, duty of care and spirit of volunteerism in both the Surf Life Saving Club (1907) and the Royal Flying Doctor Service (1928). Not a bad list, if you ask me.

As we can see, there is a whole lot more to our culture than simply cracking open cans of Foster's and throwing shrimps on the barbie. These stereotypes are based on a combination of truths and exaggerations, but ultimately do injustice to Australia's true sense of exceptionalism. Yet there are many more inspiring stories like these out there that didn't make their way into this book. In sharing these with you, I've specifically picked out the ones that I felt have had a *defining* impact on our way of life and yet happen to be not widely known. Instead, the more commercially popular stories that have gone on to form the bedrock of Australian national identity like the diggers landing at Gallipoli in 1915 — otherwise celebrated on 25th April each year as ANZAC Day — don't do justice to convey the full picture of what Australian culture and way of life are all about.

It's precisely through a couple of centuries of societal evolution that the

Australian character of mateship and sacrifice has been built. As I've argued in another essay of mine, the Australian way of life is largely centred on individualism, modesty, scepticism, personal space and strict adherence to rules.[88] Simply spelling out that these are the core ingredients that make us who we are also doesn't do full justice to the innate goodness of these values. We must point out that there are direct and tangible benefits to having these values as the core building blocks for ensuring an accountable and transparent society. The fact that we embrace individualism means that each person is free to choose their own destiny. There are cultures around the world where one may be coerced by their elders in terms of who to marry, what political beliefs to hold, what to study, what career to go into and the like. In Australia, we're all free to make our own decisions.

There are many societies where those that have wealth, status, beauty, glamour, strength or whatever else that may be commonly desired (but not necessarily possessed by most) tend to be openly boastful. In Australia, we don't usually blow our own trumpets to such a degree, nor seek to belittle others. The late Shane Warne, for instance, never referred to himself as the 'greatest' leg-spin bowler the world had ever seen in the game of cricket. It was for the commentators, the fans and his colleagues to say that. After Warne's passing, former English test cricketer and current Sky Sports commentator Nasser Hussain remarked that Warne was "the greatest ever to play the game."[89] If he had ever said those things about himself, it would've been considered arrogant.

Successful people who are 'up themselves' don't usually go down well here. Modesty is a core feature of the Australian way of life. This cultural aversion is usually looked at inversely. Rather than being seen as a case of Australians expecting their mates to not act more important than the rest, critics often interpret this expectation of self-imposed modesty as a form of jealousy. Of course, it certainly can take on that form in individual cases. There is a name for it. It's called the *Tall Poppy Syndrome* which is essentially a pejorative. It's seen as a shortcoming of the Australian cultural psyche. There is this assumption that Australians are jealous of those that are successful and get easily belittled by overt displays of personal success. As I said, there may be some elements of truth to this in select cases but as a whole, what this tendency is about is modesty. It's about ensuring that those that are smarter, wealthier, stronger, prettier, luckier, healthier, mightier and craftier than the rest don't put others down over it. When explained like this, one might appreciate that the so-called Tall Poppy Syndrome can at times be a tad misunderstood.

This somewhat excessive need to act modest to the point of self-deprecation in Australian culture means that openly boasting about anything is the quickest way to alienate folks and end up without mates. There are societies around the world where it is considered a bit more socially acceptable to boast of one's honorific titles and post-nominals as a display of social status. In Australia, that stuff is considered a form of big-noting. An Australian Dr. Joe Bloggs would usually neither expect to nor would be referred to as "Dr. Bloggs". His mates would instead just call him Joe, Joey, Joey B, JoJo, JB, Jozza, Bloggie, Bloggo, Bloggers or Bloggsie. Put it this way, there aren't many countries around the world where the heads of government are known as Scomo and Albo.

This kind of informal talk is in itself another form of equality and mateship as opposed to formal talk which is seen as a form of elitism, which is universally disliked in the Australian way of life. This is not to say that you can't be richer or brighter or more talented than the rest, just don't *act* it, unless you actually want to be thought of as a complete snob. There is an interesting observation to share on this. Many settlers from societies where openly boasting of one's own social status and achievements is considered much more tolerable tend to come to Australia, keep operating the same way and soon end up being thought of as snobbish, for essentially no fault of their own.

It's often presumed that American and Australian cultures are nearly identical. They certainly are branches of the same English-speaking tree that has its origins in the British Isles, but there are some vast differences in mentality too. One worth noting is that in America, usually any idea can find a market for itself fairly easily, from motivational speakers, to televangelists, to founders of cults, or promoters of get rich quick schemes, almost anyone can find a bunch of fans and a platform in America. It doesn't quite work the same way in Australia. We tend to be far more sceptical in our way of thinking. We dislike flowery language and lofty promises. As soon as we see someone on stage trying to offer us the solutions to all of the world's problems, that's a red flag right there, we kind of just know something smells fishy. This tendency to be sceptical of anything too dramatic is also part of the Australian mindset and way of life. This is why our political campaigns also tend to be far less combative and sensational than, for instance, the presidential debates we see in the United States. Their style of political rhetoric and theatre, while entertaining in its own right, just seems odd and a little over-the-top to Australians.

Australians enjoy giving each other personal space, both in the physical and metaphorical senses. There are societies around the world where family members, friends, acquaintances, colleagues, neighbours and the like all tend to get way too involved in people's personal lives and ask way too many nosey questions. Not only that, but often if you answer them honestly, you may be entrusting them to something private, yet the next minute they talk to someone else about you or your life, they could well end up sharing information that was supposed to be kept discreet to a gossipy mate who then ends up spreading it to your entire circle of friends. This often happens in a subconscious way without the person that does it even realising they're breaching a mate's trust. Yet this sort of a thing happens so often in certain social settings across many societies that it essentially becomes a tolerated practice by virtue of its sheer frequency. I'm not suggesting that these scenarios are impossible to find in Australian society, but they are much less prevalent. We usually keep healthy boundaries, even with our closest mates, not to be so in each other's faces all the time in case things get a bit too close for comfort, as the saying goes. Keeping that space minimises the risk of these sorts of scenarios from taking place.

In the same spirit of personal space, if we know that someone we know is going through a bit of a rut, unless they deliberately reach out for help, we don't automatically take it upon ourselves to feel obliged to weigh in on other people's personal problems. It's part of that trust we have in each other's capabilities as fellow Australians to be able to take responsibility to solve our own problems. We assume that if someone needed our help, they'd just ask and if they haven't, then they probably just want to be left alone to work it all out for themselves. By comparison, there are societies around the world where friends and family can be very pushy when it comes to imposing solutions for our problems, that make sense in their eyes but ironically not in the eyes of the very person they're trying to help. There are meddlesome folks in all societies that make everyone else's business their own, but again, this sort of a thing is generally less likely to happen in Australia.

When it comes to civil obedience, Australians have traditionally been seen as larrikins. We have often poked fun at strictness, policing and being told what to do and how to do it. Australia was, after all, the result of colonies full of convicts from the British Isles. Yet as Australian institutions have developed over the centuries, perceived and actual corruption in our government and legal spheres has become more tightly regulated and seen as morally intolerable. This is a strength of our society because from time to time, it helps us catch out someone who isn't fit for office. Equally, it can be a weakness where it goes too far and undeserving individuals end up copping the worst end of the stick. Given this landscape, there are quite a few notable examples of how difficult it has become in Australian society to survive a media scandal. A notable example was the Australia Post scandal, where Christine Holgate the CEO of a partially-funded government organisation Australia Post apparently gave expensive Cartier watches to its executives. The scandal was highly publicised and *both* Liberal and Labor governments condemned the Australia Post CEO strongly, with the then-Prime Minister Scott Morrison going so far as to remove the CEO from the position.[90] There is no shortage of other widely known examples on the public record that can easily be found on Google.

Former WA Premier Brian Burke was charged for making claims on his parliamentary account and being perceived to have put his own interests and those of his friends above the needs of the electorate.[91] Former Federal MP and House Speaker Bronwyn Bishop had to resign because she took an expensive helicopter ride and billed the taxpayer for it.[92] Former NSW Premier Barry O'Farrell had to resign because he didn't declare an expensive wine bottle as a political gift.[93] Former NSW Premier Gladys Berejiklian had to resign because she apparently used her powers in government to financially assist a fellow politician she had allegedly been in a relationship with.[94] Federal MP and then-Deputy Prime Minister Barnaby Joyce had to resign for engaging in a relationship with a staff member based on mutual consent between two consenting adults.[95]

Taken together, such incidents become proof of Australians' lack of tolerance for bending the rules, *especially* at the highest levels of power. It's true that at times, our intolerance can go too far and as a result, we've lost some good politicians just because they were plunged into a scandal without evidence. Often, tarnished reputation ends up being enough for someone to get the chop in politics. But then what's the alternative? We can't go to the other extreme and become like societies where there are next to no standards and the political class gets away with anything an average person couldn't. There are societies around the world where politicians can get away with saying and doing all sorts of dodgy things. It's all well and good to say, from the comfort of our lounge rooms, that we as a society should be somewhere in the middle as far as the threshold of tolerance goes, but easier said than done. In a choice between two extreme kinds of societies, one where politicians get away with anything and the other where they pretty much get away with nothing, it's fair to say most of us would choose the second extreme. That may well be how we need to understand the emergence of what has been dubbed 'cancel culture' in the Anglosphere and Australia certainly hasn't been exempt from its own version of this trend. It's annoying where it works against us and beneficial when it helps silence an annoying critic. It is what it is.

Moving on from that point, the other national characteristic worth noting is actually a strong sense of duty of care. Now if we see someone in trouble, we'd normally jump in to offer assistance. This has almost become like an unwritten rule of the Australian way of life. Although if people ask us for special favours that require bending the rules, we're not shy to say 'sorry mate' to our friends and move on. There are many societies around the world where friends can't take 'no' for an answer when they ask for a favour and expect you to bend the rules for them. Australia isn't that kind of a place. As larrikins, we don't really like rules, but we know when to take rules seriously. This is why we've been able to build a society where bribery, corruption, cronyism and nepotism have been minimised to a negligible level. There are societies around the world where people openly boast about being well-connected and how they could get anything they want done by making a phone call to some powerful contact of theirs. While social and professional networking for mutually beneficial relationships certainly do exist in Australia, they're not as blatant as they often are in other societies. Australia has by and large been able to get a grip on nepotistic endeavours, which is a good thing.

To wrap this up, not only does Australia have a distinct culture and way of life, it's a complex and multidimensional one, with several elements worth preserving. As far as mass immigration is concerned, Australia already had, and may continue to facilitate, these in realistic and manageable numbers.[96] Unlimited immigration causes radical demographic shifts in a country's population ratios and isn't compatible with the host nation's right to ensure its self-preservation and cultural continuity. Remember that for countries like Russia, China or India to remain fundamentally Russian, Chinese and Indian, the majority of their populations have to represent that which is authentically domestic in its character. Nobody usually bats an eyelid at the thought of those countries wanting to have restrictive immigration policies comparable to those which Australia had between 1901 and 1973. Yet if Anglosphere countries were to revert back to such policies, far too many critics would complain and launch accusations of racism. This is a double standard that's not reasonable. Either no country should have the right to ensure cultural self-preservation or all countries should have that right. That's what fairness and justice would look like. Advocating for non-Western societies to be non-settler friendly while expecting Western societies to be settler friendly is inconsistent. It only further exacerbates societal tensions. Moving forwards, the challenge for Australia's politicians will be to strike a balance between supporting diversity and ensuring that the Australian way of life is maintained for future generations to enjoy. Previous governments have too often struggled to get that balance right. We can only hope that future governments do a better job.

6

Conclusion: The Verdict

Australia has been described as many things. The lucky country. The land of opportunity. Working Man's Paradise. If the arguments presented in this book mean anything, it's clear enough by this stage that these descriptions aren't exaggerated. Lucky was the discovery of this resourceful island continent. Lucky were those early pioneers that had the chance to come here and shape the land's destiny as well as their own. For them, it was a working man's paradise. What else would be clear by this stage is that there is a lot more to this country than those vegemite and croc-hunter stereotypes that end up featuring in travel brochures. Australia is a living breathing miracle. Not enough Australians are always able to appreciate just how exceptional our country is compared to the rest of the world. Plenty of folks reckon their country is the best in the world, in our case it's actually true.

To a great extent, this lack of appreciation is attributable to a kind of cultural amnesia that disconnects modern Australians from any real appreciation for the past. Nations whose citizens are largely unaware of their own history are like an individual with no memory. The past carries the collective experiences of earlier generations, both bad and good. The left prefers to highlight the bad. The right prefers to highlight the good. Each side of the academic and political debate tries to make its own interpretation of Australia's story out to be the only truth. The left's attitude aims to achieve progress, empathy and growth from owning our bad deeds of the past and remembering them forever.

This often leads to historical revisionism and a deep sense of guilt and shame for successive generations of Australians, creating cultural hostilities and arguments that never seem to lead anywhere but towards identity politics and division. The right's attitude equally runs the risk of historical revisionism, downplaying misdeeds and errors of the past leading to a lack of responsibility and an inability to learn from our mistakes. As we've seen so far, neither attitude is preferable for modern Australians. Honest observers tend to take a realistic look at the past. This by default implies that we have to see things the way they were, rather than revising the past to suit our present-day preferences.

The cultural amnesia that results in widespread disregard for understanding our history makes us susceptible to believing a single version of it, as if that version was infallible. In recent decades, Australia has gone through a shift in its collective thought process. The end result is a lack of genuine debate about competing viewpoints. Somewhere along the way, the accusations that Australia is a 'racist' country built on 'stolen land' have managed to gain considerable popularity, not so much among the masses at large, but within the vocal minority of influencers who, despite their good intentions, often end up steering the rest of society towards counterproductive ends, while believing they're actually doing the right thing.

The beliefs that manage to spread through a community end up having far bigger consequences on the overall health and well-being of that society than what observers may realise at first sight. Widespread beliefs and public opinion form the basis of public policy in societies where the political elites wish to remain in power. They give the masses what they believe the masses wish to hear. This is why activists who wish to see change in society attempt to spread their ideas vehemently at the grassroots level. If they can get a sizable chunk of the voting public onboard with a particular viewpoint, that then becomes the new orthodoxy. The politician who desires to get into power – and stay in power – then has no choice but to embrace the orthodoxy.

If Australians are to go through a revival of attitudes towards the past and overcome that cultural amnesia, then we must start looking at history more objectively than we generally do. Too often, too many of us assume that objectivity means only telling their version of history. That's not what objectivity is. In fact, it's the opposite. If objectivity meant sitting on the fence, then no Magistrate would ever be able to hand down a verdict. An objective look at the issue would be to identify and familiarise oneself with multiple sides to an argument and then deciding which position to take as honestly as possible. Once we as a nation start doing this at the collective level, half our problem is solved.

The accusations that Australia is a racist country and that it was built on stolen land have gradually become the new orthodoxy in influential circles. Both these accusations signal a concerning implication for Australia and its future. If Australia is a racist country built on stolen land, then acknowledging it as such doesn't end the debate. It actually starts one. The activists don't suddenly hear the apologies being issued and get convinced by them. In a society with as much disregard for history as ours, the transition from a default state of indifference to the past to rapid embrace of a particular orthodoxy is quite risky. It's the equivalent of a magistrate handing down a verdict after only hearing one side of the story. Such a thing wouldn't happen in a court of law and it also shouldn't need to happen in the court of public opinion, as they say.

It is one extreme for the left to talk up the bad while talking down the good achievements in Australia's — or more generally the West's history. It is another extreme for the right to constantly talk down the bad while talking up the good achievements in our past. So far, the two sides haven't been able to reconcile their differences because each has tended to view the other as an opposing force needing to be neutralised, as if this was a zero-sum game. How we think about our past and interpret its overall essence is neither a war being fought on a battlefield nor a game being played on the sporting field where one team wins and the other loses. The left and the right's views can be reconciled and studied together in tandem. That is the only way forward.

Each of us has a past. What we list on our CVs when we apply for work covers our professional history. When we visit the local GP while being sick, what the GP pulls up on the computer screen is our medical history. When we apply for a new course at a university, the admissions team looks at our academic history. Even when we engage in personal and intimate relationships, our prospective partners in the initial stages try to understand our personal histories: who we are, what we're like, how many previous relationships we've been in and how those ended. Our past is completely interwoven into our present and our future will ultimately be shaped by both the past and the present.

Being properly aware of our professional, medical, academic or personal histories enables others to understand us and our circumstances and make the best assessment possible where shared interests are concerned. Like individuals, societies too have a past. Societies are made up of individuals who live as part of both actual and imagined communities. These communities are made up of a wide range of different 'tiers' of human identity each of which has its *own* past. In independent sovereign countries, the top tier that attempts to bind all citizens together is *national* identity and that is a product of its own interpretation of the past.

Remember that there is something fundamental that binds a Maronite Christian, a Druze and a Shi'a Muslim person together as 'Lebanese'. There is something fundamental that also binds African Americans, Hispanic Americans and Anglo-Celtic Americans together as just 'Americans'. Australia's colonial past started out ethnically and denominationally diverse with Indigenous, English, Scottish, Welsh and Irish people making up the predominant population composition of the original version of Australia during the 1800s. Over time, all of these ethnic groups essentially amalgamated into a single whole resulting in the emergence of a distinct Australian national identity by the second half of that century.

After seven decades of restrictive immigration policies between 1901 and 1973, Australia began welcoming large numbers of settlers from diverse backgrounds. By this stage, not only had Australia managed to form its own distinct mindset as an improved version of working class British culture, the question of how newcomers from non-European backgrounds would in fact find their place on Australia's national tapestry had become the subject of an on-going political debate. There weren't clear answers available to this vital question back then, as in fact there aren't today. After being able to achieve social cohesion in Australian society despite the rough and tumble experiences of the 1800s, it would be unreasonable to expect that anyone should welcome us going back to the days of social friction. We want differences to be overcome, not deepened.

Yet the more we talk ourselves down and get into the habit of playing identity politics, the less incentive there will be for newcomers from diverse backgrounds to integrate themselves into the existing culture and way of life of Australia. It's time to tell the world that overall, we're not a racist country. Over the past decade or so, Australia has taken in close to 13,000 refugees and around 190,000 newcomers each year from diverse backgrounds. Remember that people don't choose to settle in inherently racist countries. Nobody forces these people to come to Australia. The choice is made quite deliberately. The argument that the push factors are created by Western colonialism or US meddling in the domestic affairs of foreign countries has some validity on the surface, but there are plenty of developed countries that are both culturally and geographically closer to the countries of origin from which settlers come to Australia, yet they still choose Australia over those alternatives.

Observations such as these help reinforce the fact that there is something seductive about life in the West and, more specifically, in the Anglosphere, of which Australia remains an integral part. The least we may expect is that those who have chosen to call Australia home, by their own conscious will, at the very least pledge their allegiance to Australia and its national interests. Individuals may be free to practice their faith, to pass on their native tongues as second languages to their children – there are many cognitive and professional benefits to multilingualism – so long as this passing down of the native tongue doesn't happen at the expense of having native level proficiency in English at the same time. Fluency in the English language is pivotal to active participation in Australian society. Individuals may be free to introduce the diverse cuisines from their countries of origin into Australia's ever-expanding culinary repertoire, as many newcomers already have.

The ability to practise one's faith, speak one's language at home and cook one's food a certain way don't automatically pose a risk to Australia's national interests. What does are two things: One, when the newcomer is unable to pledge their allegiance and loyalty to Australia. And two, when the newcomer feels their political interests can only be represented in

Parliament by those who share their heritage or physical characteristics. These are two areas of newcomer integration into Australian society that require much greater focus to achieve balance. Many Westerners have this view that the problem with mass immigration is that some newcomers struggle to 'assimilate' into our society. The problem isn't even that.

If we look closely, some of the most troublesome individuals from overseas backgrounds have often been those that were perfectly assimilated Australians. It's usually those who sound and act Australian, who are educated at Australian public schools, who grow up with regular Australian kids kicking the footy and playing cricket that have been in intimate relationships with regular Australian partners that usually turn out to be morbidly anti-Western in their overall worldviews. This is something that hasn't been widely realised, let alone properly examined to the extent that it perhaps should. Yet it's all around us, hidden in plain sight.

During the heyday of the self-proclaimed Islamic State in Syria and Iraq (ISIS) from 2014 till its degradation by the end of the decade, the vast majority of the dual-nationals who left Anglosphere countries like Australia to join ISIS were quite Westernised in their mannerism and were perfectly assimilated into aspects of Western culture. Yet their 'Westernness' didn't stop them from joining ISIS. If anything, they used their Western-gained education and professional skills to help ISIS manage its online publications *Dabiq* and *Rumiyah* to help recruit more Westernised Muslims for the cause.[97] This criterion, which so many Westerners keep talking about the need for 'assimilation' into our society, was already met by most of the types that became foreign fighters. Worse yet, many of them were even native-born Australians of European ancestry that had converted to Islam. Melbourne teenager Jake Bilardi's story is a case in point.[98] Assimilation into Australian society doesn't stop folks from leaving to join ISIS and be at war against the West and its allies, including Australia itself.

In the same way, we find that there have been cases of activists and influencers that have often issued deeply anti-Western tweets on social media – and been widely condemned for it. This behaviour isn't usually the result of lack of assimilation into Australian society. In fact, it is an in-built feature of assimilation. Many first generation newcomers who settle in Australia from culturally distinct backgrounds are quite fond of Australia as a country, which explains why they choose to settle here in the first place. Despite whatever anti-Western views they may hold about European imperialism and US foreign policy, this first generation generally appreciates the fact that Australia has taken them in and provided them renewed opportunities to chase their dreams. It is too often the generation that grows up in Australia, assimilates into Western culture, yet remains confused about its true identity that is far more greatly predisposed to not only holding even more pronounced anti-Western views than earlier generations, in fact they're also more likely to search for a belligerent platform to release their political frustrations.

A foreign-raised newcomer is less likely to participate in any form of asymmetric warfare against the nation that has provided them a new home and a new chance at life, than a native-raised Australian of foreign origin who can't work out where their loyalty lies. This is the exact reason why I don't place a heavy emphasis on 'assimilation' as a necessary prerequisite for newcomers settling into Australian society. If we had to pick one over the other, most Australians would prefer the loyal but foreign-sounding, foreign-dressing, unassimilated person over a disloyal, local-sounding, local-dressing, assimilated one with anti-Western views.

Pledging one's allegiance to Australia, being a loyal citizen and accepting candidates regardless of their background as one's local voice to Parliament are the key to Australia continuing to remain the most successful multi-ethnic society many believe it to be at present. Members of virtually all nationalities, ethnicities, religions and sects have been able to call Australia home. Regardless of that, Australia has its own distinct identity, culture and way of life. We don't expect newcomers to blindly conform to absolutely every single aspect of our culture with their eyes closed. We don't even agree with every single aspect of our own culture ourselves. As a result, we're constantly torn from within as can be seen in the on-going debates about gender, marriage, abortion, euthanasia, drugs and the role of religion. Yet what we do expect of newcomers is the ability to be comfortable with racially impartial political representation and unflinching loyalty to Australia's national interest. This isn't much to ask for in exchange for an opportunity to settle in the greatest society on the planet and to be able to chase and fulfil one's dreams.

Let's be clear here, Australia isn't a perfect country. Its past isn't perfect. Its present isn't perfect. Its future won't be perfect. Perfection has bugger all to do with anything. For fairness, all judgements on all societies have to be relative to global standards. When we look at Australia through a comparative lens, we find that both its discovery (1770) and its settlement (1788) by the British Empire were entirely consistent with the global political and legal norms of the timeframe in which they took place. As we discussed, the British were not intentionally malevolent towards Indigenous Australians. Their original instructions were to maximise their territorial gains with the consent of the natives, as regimes who had the means to do so in those days commonly used to do. We must avoid judging the past according to present-day norms. In this case, doing so would be anachronistic, counterproductive and misleading all at once.

As we saw, territorial acquisition by the use of force was only prohibited after World War II in 1945 when the United Nations' Charter was issued. This prohibition was not to apply retroactively and the year of the signing of the Kellogg-Briand Pact which was 1928 became the commonly understood cut-off for demarcating legitimate conquests. Since Australia was claimed in 1770 by Captain Cook with no central authority to negotiate with and was settled from 1788 onwards, which is 140 years before the cut-off, that makes Australia's settlement perfectly legitimate by the rules of the old world order. Land theft has bugger all to do with anything. Besides, all lands in the world have at some point been conquered and re-conquered throughout history. There is little value in singling out the West's conquests as the worst cases of the lot.

Australia is a country on a journey to better itself in gradual steps. It's true that accounts of Australia's colonisation were a mixed bag in terms of relations between settlers and natives. This has been discussed at some length in this book. Yet if one observation is clear, it's that this journey towards self-improvement started almost as quickly as the First Fleet landing in Sydney. Remember the social, cultural and political backdrop we went through about English society in the late 1700s and early 1800s were one made up of a rigid class structure. The ruling elites were seen as 'snobs'. Yet convict duo Henry Kable and Susannah Holmes were able to sue their ship Captain on board HMS Alexander for lost luggage and win £15 in compensation. This story of Australia's commitment to rule of law and equality remains as central today as it was in 1788.

Much of Australia's identity and way of life that we take for granted today came about during that formative century — the 1800s. These little known defining moments from our past serve as counter-arguments to the oft-repeated criticism that we don't even have a culture or way of life worth preserving. This unreasonable view is often cited by the advocates of importing cultural diversity through open borders on the basis that since we don't have our own culture, what are we even at risk of losing in the first place? This is something we have tackled in this book. The challenge for a good historian is not what to include in the next piece of work, rather it is the ability to work out what to exclude. It is the ability to make this judgement without doing injustice to the topic at hand is the greatest challenge. This is a challenge I hope was confronted with grace and wisdom during the authorship of this book.

I've consistently reminded us that this isn't a history textbook. Rather, it's a book that addresses some issues that have become central to Australia's future and way of life. These are issues such as the accusations that Australia is a racist country, that it is built on stolen land and that it doesn't even have a culture. In responding to these accusations, all of which hold concerning implications for the country's future, this book has had to draw to your attention a select range of very specific developments in our journey that have gone on to define our values.

These developments are the reason for our unique culture and way of life. Be it Andrew Bent establishing free press in 1824, or the *Church Act* in 1836 that established religious tolerance, or the Eureka Stockade in 1854 that established a fair go for workers, or the advent of the Secret Ballot in 1854 that established political privacy and freedom of association, or the Indigenous cricket team in 1868 that laid the foundations for racial equality in sports, or the *Commonwealth Franchise Act* in 1902 that established gender equality in our democracy, or the Surf Life Saving Club in 1907 and the Royal Flying Doctor Service in 1928 both of which established duty of care and the spirit of volunteerism, these unique defining moments make us, us.

It is through these experiences — and many like them not otherwise covered in this book — pioneered by earlier generations, that Australia became an improved version of working class British society from the 1800s. Coming to terms with these fascinating aspects of our history helps us dispel so many commonly-assumed myths about us. In particular, the oft-repeated accusation that we don't even have a culture worth saving. It's clear here that we do. It is a culture based on equality, free press, religious tolerance, fair go, privacy, democracy, freedom of association, racial equality, gender equality, duty of care and the spirit of volunteerism. No one here is claiming that this culture is perfect, nor are we claiming that it should forever remain stubbornly opposed to change. It is true that cultures do evolve over time, sometimes to better ends and other times to worse ends. They often change in response to the economic, technological and political challenges of the day which may otherwise be difficult to predict, let alone navigate in advance.

When the need for change arises, the society has to have a conversation with itself, entertain free and frank debates within bounds of respect and see what consensus can be formed. This is not a perfect system. I realise the consensus view isn't always the right view. Yet doing it this way just about beats any alternatives. It should suffice until humanity figures out a less unreliable way to tackle cultural change over time. Now, even for such free and frank debates to take place, there has to be a central cultural core that facilitates this process. That core for us is made up of many of the fundamentals discussed in this book. Change for the sake of change is too great a risk for the well-being of a society. Our natural inclination should be to preserve the essence of what we have. Any proposed cultural change, or shift in norms, should be critically examined before deciding whether or not to allow it to be normalised. In theory, this is what Australia already does. In practice, one side of the debate is often given greater emphasis by the influencers than the other and those who disagree can sometimes be ostracised. The challenge is working out the right balance between healthy self-preservation and transitioning to the future which will inevitably result in more societal evolution. That is something we as Australians need to have a good long think about.

Let's also be clear that when we speak of racial equality as one of our core values, we're not pretending that we have ever got it spot on from the beginning. No society has and Australia shouldn't be held to a different standard compared to other places. The early principles of racial equality in Australia could be traced back to examples such as the issuing of Letters Patent establishing the Province of South Australia in 1836, in which British authorities specified the recognition of the rights of Indigenous peoples inhabiting South Australia at the time. Or in 1868, with the Indigenous cricket team representing us in England. In any case, there were many other instances of systemic discrimination against Indigenous Australians that took a century to correct. This is why the Menzies Liberal government had a law passed in 1962 to give all Indigenous Australians and Torres Strait Islanders the right to vote at federal elections. By 1965, the same right had been extended across every state. Finally, in May 1967, the Holt Liberal government put the question to the Australian public in an open referendum whether they supported the idea of changing Section 51 (xxvi) of the Commonwealth constitution to enable Australia to make laws for all people equally and Section 127 was removed so that all Australians would be counted as part of the census. A resounding 91 per cent of Australians voted 'Yes'. This sort of self-induced 'course correction' doesn't happen in racist societies.

There are many more conciliatory measures pursued by both sides of politics in Australia than what has been covered in the finite chapters of this book. Yet none of these positive developments like the reforms of the 1960s are widely discussed let alone celebrated. Instead, the public discussion tends to focus disproportionately on the past and present friction between Indigenous and non-Indigenous Australians. Pitched against the backdrop of a population that is largely indifferent to the past, it doesn't take long before these kinds of narratives start to permeate the consciousness of Australians far and wide. What isn't supposed to be a suburban Australian trend ends up appearing like one at the dictate of a minority of academics and activists wanting to present a one-sided view of Australia's story.

I'm usually not one to presume bad faith on the part of those whose political beliefs and values don't align with my own. I believe that when academics and activists, who happen to be in the other school of thought, claim colonisation was bad, some are doing so in good faith and out of genuine empathy for Indigenous Australians. Just because some of us believe their advocacy is often counterproductive or that their diagnosis of the problem is one-sided, that is not always a good reason to question their motives or intentions. A large part of the reason why these debates in Australia's academic, media and political circles haven't been able to find any common ground is because those who participate in them usually lack mutual trust. They constantly accuse each other of making things up, which is basically accusing someone of being a liar, or they would accuse each other of 'cancelling' opinions they disagree with. These sorts of tactics undermine our capacity to be able to engage in civilised debates on sensitive issues.

Be that as it may, through the endless screaming out of one opinion over another, somehow something that does look like a consensus view has begun to emerge. That view of Australia more or less makes Australia's European heritage and more specifically its British Isles component out to be inherently racist. As we've seen throughout this book, racism is an elusive concept to define at best and not nearly as widespread as its critics often make it out to be. It isn't the regular practice for most world societies to have anti-racism laws in place. Australia does. It has many state and federal laws to combat racism. Many feel that some pieces of supposed anti-racism legislation such as Section 18C of the *Racial Discrimination Act* (1975) go a step too far in their quest to quarantine our society from racism. But in any case, the fact that such legislation even exists in the first place absolves Australia of the accusation that it is a systemically racist country, or that it has a culture that is racist.

The bottom line is, Australia is a great country and for it to be able to continue to be great, it will require national cohesion and consciousness that brings everyone together on the journey regardless of race. Like any independent state, Australia will end up struggling to survive without an identity that the majority of its inhabitants can connect with and a way of life that the majority of its citizens feel they can call theirs. It is precisely the fact that Australian culture is based on things like individualism, modesty, scepticism, personal space and a strict adherence to rules that we are able to minimise the sort of corruption, bribery and nepotism that is rampant across many other parts of the world. This is our story, imperfect but constantly improving. These are our values, imperfect but able to minimise the ills other parts of the world struggle to get a grip on. It is no wonder so many choose to come here entirely off their own accord. Without a doubt, we should do all we can to preserve this way of life. Our political class should be promoting integrity and calling to unite all Australian citizens under our shared values.

Despite Australia being exceptional as it is, its virtues — of which there are so many — aren't discussed often enough. Meanwhile, its vices — of which there are some — are discussed all too often. The accusations that Australia has no culture of its own, that it is a 'racist' country built on 'stolen land' have now become so widespread and so normalised that there was a need for this book to be written. Put it this way, the referendum held in October 2023 was essentially a direct consequence of these beliefs being left unchallenged for far too long. The relationship between beliefs and policies is an undeniable one. I'm not suggesting though that these beliefs about Australia being a racist country built on stolen land was necessarily the default position within the ordinary public. The public was largely apathetic about this stuff. It was a minority of activists and their supporters who conjured up this idea that Indigenous Australians needed to have their own constitutionally enshrined advisory body to the government of the day. That now-settled Voice proposal had been in the making for some time. But it should be put behind us and allow the nation room for healing.

There is a tier of our society where the so-called 'history wars'[99] and 'culture wars' have been debated at length. That tier features what may appear to a bystander like an apocalyptic struggle between just about every mainstream historian and the lone voice of Keith Windschuttle. That debate is taking place in an arena that is way too highbrow of normal Australians. Like most debates among academics, that stuff is also too detailed and far too technical to stand any chance of having a real impact on public opinion. That process lacks any real prospects of ever reaching normal Australians, let alone help make them become better informed.

Academic discussions can sometimes be distant from everyday realities, but their underlying issues matter to us all. It is with a vision to make these debates accessible and relatable to everyday Australians that I decided to write this book. I sought to present contentious issues facing our nation in plain language, away from academic jargon, and offer a thorough understanding of the challenges and accusations we face. Australia can overcome its cultural amnesia by cultivating a deeper interest in its rich and varied national story. While we have had our share of issues, Australia, at its core, is not a fundamentally racist country, nor was its settlement upon stolen land and it does have a way of life worth celebrating. These assertions may spark debate, but that's not a bad thing. In writing this book, my objective was to contribute to the continuous project of improving our great nation by offering balanced perspectives. I hope that this work has provided you, the reader, with valuable insights and inspired you to join in our shared quest to maintain this balance. As we navigate and make sense of the critical debates of our time, it is my hope that we continue to celebrate Australia's unique identity and together advance towards an enriching, unified and free future that embodies the best aspects of the Australian way of life.

Endnotes

1   https://www.news.com.au/travel/australian-holidays/what-foreigners-really-think-of-australians/news-story/e3e9f31b2518ac5b6eac9378a2c709f3

2   https://www.vice.com/en/article/d7egea/talking-to-people-who-have-zero-interest-in-leaving-australia

3   https://eastasiaforum.org/2023/12/12/imagining-a-migration-system-for-australias-future/

4   Lee, M. A. (2007). *A Fair Go: Race Politics and Public Discourse in Australia.* VDM Verlag Dr. Müller, p.73

5   https://www.youtube.com/watch?v=wkGEMYSgIo0

6   https://www.youtube.com/watch?v=OdCkB-2_7EU

7   https://www.skynews.com.au/world-news/dont-let-your-guard-down-the-islamist-terror-threat-is-as-real-as-ever-21-years-on-from-the-911-attacks-that-shocked-the-world/news-story/c0a6cb39a501f005f62ee008914242ab

8   Anderson, B. (2006). *Imagined Communities.* Verso, p.6

9   *The World Book Encyclopedia.* (1981). World Book-Childcraft International, p.792

10   https://www.latimes.com/entertainment-arts/movies/story/2023-08-04/oppenheimer-movie-christopher-nolan-atomic-bomb-hiroshima-nagasaki-critics

11   https://www.spiked-online.com/2017/12/01/hollywoods-race-war/

12   https://www.abc.net.au/news/2020-05-28/minneapolis-george-floyd-protests-amplify-bad-us-race-relations/12294626

13   https://www.washingtonpost.com/politics/how-donald-trump-came-up-with-make-america-great-again/2017/01/17/fb6acf5e-dbf7-11e6-ad42-f3375f271c9c_story.html

14   O'Brien, J. M. (Ed.). (2021). *The Oxford Handbook of the Minor Prophets.* Oxford University Press., p.313

15   *The United Nations, NATO, and the Former Yugoslavia: Hearing Before the Commission on Security and Cooperation in Europe, One Hundred Fourth Congress, First Session, April 6, 1995.* (1995). U.S. Government Printing Office, p.64

16   Said, E. W. (1995). *Orientalism.* Penguin Group, p.73

17   Nager, B. R. (2010). *And Be Free.* Xlibris Corporation LLC, p.18

18   Clark, A. (2022). *Making Australian History.* Vintage, p.121

19   https://www.theguardian.com/australia-news/2022/aug/21/what-is-an-indigenous-treaty-and-how-would-it-work-in-australia

20   https://www.skynews.com.au/opinion/dear-lidia-thorpe-the-queen-is-no-coloniser-she-dissolved-her-empires-overseas-outposts-like-no-other-world-leader/news-story/209eb214df8d54f34d29a8012250934d

21   Pilkington, D. (2013). *Follow the Rabbit-Proof Fence.* University of Queensland Press, p.16

22   Karl, R. E. (2010). *Mao Zedong and China in the Twentieth-Century World: A Concise History.* Duke University Press, p.118

23   https://www.greenleft.org.au/content/lidia-thorpe-sovereignty-has-never-been-ceded

24   https://www.smh.com.au/national/shouty-uninformed-ineffective-how-senator-lidia-thorpe-annoys-the-establishment-20220323-p5a73j.html

25   Cronin, D. (2021). *Trapped by History.* Rowman & Littlefield, p.200

26 Hassan, A., & Barber, S. J. (2021). *The effects of repetition frequency on the illusory truth effect. Cognitive Research: Principles and Implications*, 6(1), p.1

27 Baudrillard, J. (1994). *Simulacra and Simulation*. University of Michigan Press, p.27

28 https://www.news.com.au/national/why-australia-day-has-to-change-from-january-26/news-story/e9cc240a65f3da20ada71ef0dfae79ca

29 https://www.abc.net.au/news/2014-05-13/goodes-gets-behind-public-campaign-for-constitutional-recogniti/5450422

30 https://www.theguardian.com/australia-news/2022/aug/21/what-is-an-indigenous-treaty-and-how-would-it-work-in-australia

31 https://theconversation.com/a-constitutional-voice-to-parliament-ensuring-parliament-is-in-charge-not-the-courts-193017

32 Cairns, R., & Gerrard, K. (2020). *Flatlining? National Enrolment Trends in Senior Secondary History*. Agora, p.63

33 https://www2.sl.nsw.gov.au/archive/events/exhibitions/2006/firstsight/docs/firstsight_guide.pdf

34 https://www.britishempire.co.uk/maproom/dampiersvoyages.htm

35 Blainey, G. (2020). *Captain Cook's Epic Voyage*. Penguin Random House Australia, p.2

36 Keegan, N. M. (2018). *Early Colonial History and American Independence. In US Consular Representation in Britain since 1790* (pp. 9–12). Anthem Press.

37 Herrington, S. (2014). "The Forests of Canada: Seeing the Forests for the Trees", in F. Uekötter & U. Lübken (Eds.), *Managing the Unknown: Essays on Environmental Ignorance* (1st ed., pp. 53–70). Berghahn Books.

38 https://www.thehistorypress.co.uk/articles/transportation-to-australia/

39 Sharman, J. C. (2019). *Company Sovereigns and the Empires of the East. In Empires of the Weak: The Real Story of European Expansion and the Creation of the New World Order* (pp. 65–98). Princeton University Press.

40 MacPhail, M., & Owen, T. (2018). "What was growing along the Tank Stream Valley, Sydney Cove, in 1788?", *Australasian Historical Archaeology*, 36, pp.16–28

41 Teo, H. M. (2021). "Transported for life, transported by love: love and the Australian convict romance novel", in *The Routledge Companion to Romantic Love* (pp. 191-202). Routledge.

42 https://www.theguardian.com/sport/2018/jun/05/the-spin-aboriginal-xi-celebratory-tour-cricket

43 Blainey, G. (1966). *The Tyranny of Distance: How distance shaped Australia's history*. Sun Books.

44 Dhuga, U. S. (2016). "Not Me Go to England No More": Michael Farrell's Writing Australian Unsettlement. *Antipodes*, 30(1), pp.206–207

45 Lawrence, S., & Davies, P. (2017). *Liquid Asset: Water in Victorian Gold Mining. RCC Perspectives*, 2, p.71

46 Rickard, J. (2017). *Australia: A Cultural History*. Monash University, p.70

47 Sufi, S. (2019). *The Linguistic Roots of Nationalism*. Connor Court, p.25

48 Rodney, W. (2018). *How Europe Underdeveloped Africa*. Verso Books, p.162

49 Karsh, E. (2007). *Islamic Imperialism: A History*. Yale University Press, p.65

50 Bromark, S., & Leong, H. K. (2014). *Four Hundred Years after the Battle of Vienna. In Massacre in Norway: The 2011 Terror Attacks on Oslo and the Utøya Youth Camp* (pp. 56–66). University of Nebraska Press.

51 Wright, C. A. (2007). *The Medieval Spice Trade and the Diffusion of the Chile*. Gastronomica, 7(2), pp.35–43

52   https://www.filmsite.org/epicsfilms3.html

53   Yao, J. (2022). "The 1815 Congress of Vienna and the oldest continuous interstate institution", in *The ideal river* (pp. 63-83). Manchester University Press.

54   Pettitt, C. (2022). *Serial Revolutions 1848: Writing, Politics, Form.* Oxford University Press, p.1

55   Strachwitz, R. (2022). *The Theory of the Public Sphere Revisited. In Civil Society: Concepts, Challenges, Contexts* (pp. 31-49). Springer, Cham.

56   Ross, J. (2014). *Forecast for D-Day: And the Weatherman Behind Ike's Greatest Gamble.* Lyons Press, p.88

57   Scarfi, J. P. (2022). "Francisco de Vitoria and the (geo) politics of canonisation in Spain/America". *Leiden Journal of International Law*, pp.1-17

58   Rogers, D. (2022). *Wars, Laws, Rights and the Making of Global Insecurities.* Springer International Publishing, p.37

59   https://www.un.org/securitycouncil/content/purposes-and-principles-un-chapter-i-un-charter#rel2

60   Hathaway, O., Shapiro, S. (2017). *The Internationalists: And Their Plan to Outlaw War.* Penguin Books Limited.

61   https://pursuit.unimelb.edu.au/articles/how-does-the-international-court-of-justice-differ-from-the-international-criminal-court

62   Csurgai, G. (2020). *Geopolitics, Geostrategy and Geoeconomics: Reflections on the Changing Force Factors in the International System. Economic Strategies*, 144, p.36

63   Vine, D. (2021). *The United States of War: A Global History of America's Endless Conflicts, from Columbus to the Islamic State.* University of California Press.

64   Kanekar, A. (2022). *Architecture, Nationalism, and the Fleeting Heyday of the Goan Temple.* Kritika Kultura, 38, pp.455-481

65   Loizides, N., Psaltis, C., Morgan-Jones, E., Sudulich, L., Popp, R., & Baykiz, T. (2022). "Citizens and Peace Mediations in Divided Societies: Identifying Zones of Agreement through a Conjoint Survey Experiment". *Journal of Conflict Resolution*, 66(9), p.1619

66   https://edition.cnn.com/2023/10/08/middleeast/israel-gaza-attack-hostages-response-intl-hnk/index.html

67   https://www.theguardian.com/commentisfree/2022/feb/28/nato-expansion-war-russia-ukraine

68   https://www.aljazeera.com/news/2022/3/9/smells-of-genocide-how-putin-justifies-russias-war-in-ukraine

69   https://www.newyorker.com/magazine/2017/09/18/what-happens-when-war-is-outlawed

70   Banner, S. (2005). "Why Terra Nullius? Anthropology and Property Law in Early Australia". *Law and History Review*, 23(1), p.103

71   Egan, R. (2021). *Power and Dysfunction: The New South Wales Board for the Protection of Aborigines 1883–1940.* Australian National University Press, p.21

72   https://theconversation.com/lidia-thorpe-wants-to-shift-course-on-indigenous-recognition-heres-why-we-must-respect-the-uluru-statement-141609

73   https://www.theage.com.au/national/oi-no-such-thing-as-australian-values-20180629-p4zojc.html

74   Hansson, A. (1996). *Chinese Outcasts: Discrimination and Emancipation in Late Imperial China.* E.J. Brill, p.20

75   Ninan, M. M. (2018). *Ambedkar's Philosophy of Hinduism and Contemporary Critiques.* Lulu Press, p.190

76 *The Australian Encyclopaedia: Ferns to Ley.* (1977). Grolier Society of Australia, p.438

77 Woodberry, J. (1972). *Andrew Bent and the Freedom of the Press in Van Diemen's Land*. Fullers Bookshop, p.53

78 Carey, H. M. (2011). *God's Empire: Religion and Colonialism in the British World, C.1801–1908*. Cambridge University Press, pp.11-12

79 https://www.nma.gov.au/defining-moments/resources/eureka-stockade

80 Grey, J. (2008). *A Military History of Australia*. Cambridge University Press, p.18

81 https://www.aph.gov.au/About_Parliament/Senate/Powers_practice_n_procedures/pops/pop37/sawer

82 https://www.sl.nsw.gov.au/stories/first-indigenous-cricket-tour-england-1868

83 https://artsandculture.google.com/story/1866-melbourne-cricket-club-v-indigenous-xi-cricket-australia/cAVhE7n_D8_tIQ?hl=en

84 https://theconversation.com/australian-politics-explainer-how-women-gained-the-right-to-vote-74080

85 https://www.spectator.com.au/2022/02/115-years-of-the-bondi-surf-bathers-life-saving-club/

86 https://www.dailytelegraph.com.au/newslocal/northern-beaches/queenscliff-surf-life-saving-club-proud-to-hear-mike-baird-set-to-be-premier/news-story/665 2d75b95019c272e5df9c0084b6b57

87 https://www.abc.net.au/news/2018-08-16/royal-flying-doctor-service-at-national-museum/10122320

88 Wild, D., Finlay, L., Sufi, S., Pawle, F., Gorman, Z., Abbott, T., Creighton, A., Foster, G., & Hussey, C. (2021). *Essays for Australia* - Volume 1 2021. Institute of Public Affairs, p.42

89 https://www.skysports.com/cricket/news/12080/12557974/shane-warne-the-greatest-to-ever-play-the-game-says-nasser-hussain

90 https://www.afr.com/politics/federal/huge-explosion-as-caribbean-volcano-blows-20210413-p57imu

91 https://www.perthnow.com.au/news/wa/brian-burke-memoir-a-tumultuous-life-set-to-ruffle-wa-politics-ng-306994a40489a3a52bec6599c8d0e61a

92 https://www.abc.net.au/news/2015-08-02/bronwyn-bishop-stands-down-as-speaker/6666172

93 https://www.theguardian.com/world/2014/apr/16/barry-ofarrell-resigns-as-nsw-premier-after-thankyou-card-for-wine-emerges

94 https://www.smh.com.au/politics/nsw/berejiklian-was-right-to-resign-but-her-conduct-was-not-criminal-20230628-p5dk26.html

95 https://www.abc.net.au/news/2018-02-23/barnaby-joyce-resigns/9477942

96 https://www.theaustralian.com.au/commentary/opinion/multiculturalism-has-failed-lets-cut-immigration-refugee-intake/news-story/7939b6160685f98c2fb3d6 e404b6d422

97 Azani, E., & Dotti, F. (2021). *The Islamic State's Web Jihadi Magazine Dabiq and Rumiyah: More than just Propaganda*. International Institute for Counter-Terrorism (ICT), p.6

98 https://www.bbc.com/news/world-australia-31845428

99 Munro, D. (2021). *History Wars*. ANU Press, p.18

Bibliography

ABC News. (2015, August 2). *Bronwyn Bishop resigns as Speaker: Tony Abbott announces review of entitlements system*. ABC News. https://www.abc.net.au/news/2015-08-02/bronwyn-bishop-stands-down-as-speaker/6666172

Aldred, T. (2018, June 5). *In the Footsteps of their Ancestors: Aboriginal XI begin Celebratory Tour*. The Guardian. https://www.theguardian.com/sport/2018/jun/05/the-spin-aboriginal-xi-celebratory-tour-cricket

Allam, L. (2022, August 21). *What is an Indigenous treaty and how would it work in Australia?* The Guardian. https://www.theguardian.com/australia-news/2022/aug/21/what-is-an-indigenous-treaty-and-how-would-it-work-in-australia

Al-Jazeera. (2022, March 9). *'Smells of Genocide': How Putin justifies Russia's war in Ukraine*. Al-Jazeera. https://www.aljazeera.com/news/2022/3/9/smells-of-genocide-how-putin-justifies-russias-war-in-ukraine

Anderson, B. (2006). *Imagined Communities*. Verso.

Australian Institute of Aboriginal and Torres Strait Islander Studies. (2021, April 15). *The 1967 Referendum. Australian Institute of Aboriginal and Torres Strait Islander Studies*. Australian Institute of Aboriginal and Torres Strait Islander Studies. https://aiatsis.gov.au/explore/1967-referendum

Azani, E., & Dotti, F. (2021). *The Islamic State's Web Jihadi Magazine Dabiq and Rumiyah: More than just Propaganda*. International Institute for Counter-Terrorism (ICT). http://www.jstor.org/stable/resrep37748

Banner, S. (2005). Why Terra Nullius? Anthropology and Property Law in Early Australia. *Law and History Review*, 23(1), 95–131.

http://www.jstor.org/stable/30042845

Baudrillard, J. (1994). *Simulacra and Simulation.* University of Michigan Press.

BBC News. (2015, March 12). *Jake Bilardi: The radicalisation of an Australian teen.* BBC News. https://www.bbc.com/news/world-australia-31845428

Blainey, G. (1966). *The Tyranny of Distance: How distance shaped Australia's history.* Sun Books.

Blainey, G. (2020). *Captain Cook's Epic Voyage.* Penguin Random House Australia.

Boucher, A. (2023, December 12). *Imagining a migration system for Australia's future.* East Asia Forum. https://eastasiaforum.org/2023/12/12/imagining-a-migration-system-for-australias-future/

Bromark, S., & Leong, H. K. (2014). *Massacre in Norway: The 2011 Terror Attacks on Oslo and the Utuya Youth Camp.* University of Nebraska Press. https://doi.org/10.2307/j.ctt1d9nmsn.8

Burdon, A. (Ed.). (2006, March). *First Sight - The Dutch Mapping of Australia 1606-1697.* State Library of New South Wales. https://www2.sl.nsw.gov.au/archive/events/exhibitions/2006/firstsight/docs/firstsight_guide.pdf

Carey, H. M. (2011). *God's Empire: Religion and Colonialism in the British World, C.1801–1908.* Cambridge University Press.

Carpenter, T. G. (2022, February 28). *Many predicted NATO expansion would lead to war. Those warnings were ignored.* The Guardian. https://www.theguardian.com/commentisfree/2022/feb/28/nato-expansion-war-russia-ukraine

Cairns, R., & Gerrard, K. (2020). *Flatlining? National Enrolment Trends in Senior Secondary History.* Agora.

Clark, A. (2022). *Making Australian History.* Vintage.

Collins, A. (2014, May 13). *Goodes urges support for constitutional change*. ABC News. https://www.abc.net.au/news/2014-05-13/goodes-gets-behind-public-campaign-for-constitutional-recogniti/5450422

Cricket Australia. (2011). *Who was Australia's first Prime Minister?* [Video]. YouTube. https://www.youtube.com/watch?v=OdCkB-2_7EU

Cronin, D. (2021). *Trapped by History.* Rowman & Littlefield.

Csurgai, G. (2020). Geopolitics, Geostrategy and Geoeconomics: Reflections on the Changing Force Factors in the International System. *Economic Strategies,* 144, 30-41. https://doi.org/10.33917/es-3.169.2020.30-41

Dhuga, U. S. (2016). "Not Me Go to England No More": Michael Farrell's Writing Australian Unsettlement. *Antipodes,* 30(1), 206–220. https://doi.org/10.13110/antipodes.30.1.0206

Diss, K. (2020, May 28). *In America, a bystander with a smartphone bears witness, but cannot deliver justice. George Floyd's death shows the power of social media as the US continues to grapple with racial tensions.* ABC News. https://www.abc.net.au/news/2020-05-28/minneapolis-george-floyd-protests-amplify-bad-us-race-relations/12294626

Filmsite LLC. (n.d.). Epics - Historical Films. https://www.filmsite.org/epicsfilms3.html

Egan, R. (2021). *Power and Dysfunction: The New South Wales Board for the Protection of Aborigines 1883–1940.* Australian National University Press.

Gold, H., Faqiri, S., Regan, H., Yeung, J., & Hu, C. (2023, October 9). *Israel formally declares war against Hamas as it battles to push militants off its soil.* CNN. https://edition.cnn.com/2023/10/08/middleeast/israel-gaza-attack-hostages-response-intl-hnk/index.html

Google. (n.d.). *1866 Melbourne Cricket Club v indigenous XI - Google Arts & Culture.* Google Arts & Culture. https://artsandculture.google.com/story/1866-melbourne-cricket-club-v-indigenous-xi-cricket-australia/cAVhE7n_D8_tIQ?hl=en

Grey, J. (2008). *A Military History of Australia*. Cambridge University Press.

Hansson, A. (1996). *Chinese Outcasts: Discrimination and Emancipation in Late Imperial China*. E.J. Brill.

The Guardian. (2014, April 16). *Barry O'Farrell resigns as NSW Premier after thank you card for wine emerges*. The Guardian. https://www. theguardian.com/world/2014/apr/16/barry-ofarrell-resigns-as-nsw-premier-after-thankyou-card-for-wine-emerge

Hassan, A., & Barber, S. J. (2021). The effects of repetition frequency on the illusory truth effect. *Cognitive Research: Principles and Implications*, 6(1). https://doi.org/10.1186/s41235-021-00301-5

Hathaway, O., Shapiro, S. (2017). *The Internationalists: And Their Plan to Outlaw War*. Penguin Books Limited.

Herrington, S. (2014). The Forests of Canada: Seeing the Forests for the Trees. In F. Uekötter & U. Lübken (Eds.), *Managing the Unknown: Essays on Environmental Ignorance* (1st ed., pp. 53–70). Berghahn Books.

Hussain, N. (2022, March 6). *Shane Warne "the greatest to ever play the game" says Nasser Hussain*. Sky Sports. https://www.skysports.com/cricket/news/12080/12557974/shane-warne-the-greatest-to-ever-play-the-game-says-nasser-hussain

ilovemytele2000. (2016). *Centenary of Federation - Edmund Barton (1999)* [Video]. YouTube. https://www.youtube.com/watch?v=wkGEMYSgIo0

Kanekar, A. (2022). *Architecture, Nationalism, and the Fleeting Heyday of the Goan Temple*. Kritika Kultura.

Karl, R. E. (2010). *Mao Zedong and China in the Twentieth-Century World: A Concise History*. Duke University Press.

Karsh, E. (2007). *Islamic Imperialism: A History*. Yale University Press

Keating, J. (2022, September 27). *Australian politics explainer: How women gained the right to vote.* The Conversation. https://theconversation.com/australian-politics-explainer-how-women-gained-the-right-to-vote-74080

Keegan, N. M. (2018). *Early Colonial History and American Independence. In US Consular Representation in Britain since 1790* (pp. 9–12). Anthem Press.

Larkin, D., & Maguire, A. (2023, January 17). *Lidia Thorpe wants to shift course on indigenous recognition. Here's why we must respect the Uluru statement.* The Conversation. https://theconversation.com/lidia-thorpe-wants-to-shift-course-on-indigenous-recognition-heres-why-we-must-respect-the-uluru-statement-141609

Latimore, J. (2022, April 24). *"Shouty, uninformed, ineffective": How Senator Lidia Thorpe annoys the establishment.* The Sydney Morning Herald. https://www.smh.com.au/national/shouty-uninformed-ineffective-how-senator-lidia-thorpe-annoys-the-establishment-20220323-p5a73j.html

Lawrence, S., & Davies, P. (2017). Liquid Asset: Water in Victorian Gold Mining. *RCC Perspectives, 2,* 71–80. http://www.jstor.org/stable/26241434

Lee, M. A. (2007). *A Fair Go: Race Politics and Public Discourse in Australia.* VDM Verlag Dr. Müller.

Loizides, N., Psaltis, C., Morgan-Jones, E., Sudulich, L., Popp, R., & Baykiz, T. (2022). Citizens and Peace Mediations in Divided Societies: Identifying Zones of Agreement through a Conjoint Survey Experiment. *Journal of Conflict Resolution,* 66(9), 1619–1649. https://doi.org/10.1177/00220027221108221

MacPhail, M., & Owen, T. (2018). *What was growing along the Tank Stream Valley, Sydney Cove, in 1788?.* Australasian Historical Archaeology.

Maher, L. (2018, August 16). *Flying doctor artefacts land at museum to highlight its enduring role.* ABC News. https://www.abc.net.au/news/2018-08-16/royal-flying-doctor-service-at-national-museum/1012232.

McIntyre, J. (2024, January 19). *How does the International Court of Justice differ from the International Criminal Court?*. Pursuit. https://pursuit.unimelb.edu.au/articles/how-does-the-international-court-of-justice-differ-from-the-international-criminal-court

Menand, L. (2017, September 11). *What happens when war is outlawed.* The New Yorker. https://www.newyorker.com/magazine/2017/09/18/what-happens-when-war-is-outlawed

Mitchell, S. (2020, December 20). *What foreigners really think of Australians.* News.com.au. https://www.news.com.au/travel/australian-holidays/what-foreigners-really-think-of-australians/news-story/e3e9f31b2518ac5b6eac9378a2c709f3

Moore, T., Rudra, N., & Boddy, N. (2021, April 13). *"Utter disgrace": Holgate continues to lash PM.* Australian Financial Review. https://www.afr.com/politics/federal/huge-explosion-as-caribbean-volcano-blows-20210413-p57imu

Morris, S. (2022, October 27). *A constitutional voice to parliament: Ensuring parliament is in charge, not the courts.* The Conversation. https://theconversation.com/a-constitutional-voice-to-parliament-ensuring-parliament-is-in-charge-not-the-courts-193017

Munro, D. (2021) *History Wars.* ANU Press.

Nager, B. R. (2010). *And Be Free.* Xlibris Corporation LLC.

National Museum of Australia. (2023, May 26). *Eureka Stockade.* National Museum of Australia. https://www.nma.gov.au/defining-moments/resources/eureka-stockade

Ninan, M. M. (2018). *Ambedkar's Philosophy of Hinduism and Contemporary Critiques.* Lulu Press.

O'Reilly, J. (2017, February 28). *Why some people have zero interest in leaving Australia.* VICE. https://www.vice.com/en/article/d7egea/talking-to-people-who-have-zero-interest-in-leaving-australia

Parri, L. (2017, January 22). *Brian Burke memoir A Tumultuous Life set to ruffle WA politics.* PerthNow. https://www.perthnow.com.au/news/wa/brian-burke-memoir-a-tumultuous-life-set-to-ruffle-wa-politics-ng-306994a40489a3a52bec6599c8d0e61a

Pettitt, C. (2022). *Serial Revolutions 1848: Writing, Politics, Form.* Oxford University Press.

Pilkington, D. (2013). *Follow the Rabbit-Proof Fence.* University of Queensland Press.

Rickard, J. (2017) *Australia: A Cultural History.* Monash University

Rodney, W. (2018). *How Europe Underdeveloped Africa.* Verso Books.

Rogers, D. (2022). *Wars, Laws, Rights and the Making of Global Insecurities.* Springer International Publishing.

Ross, J. (2014). *Forecast for D-Day: And the Weatherman Behind Ike's Greatest Gamble.* Lyons Press.

Said, E. W. (1995). *Orientalism.* Penguin Group.

Sawer, M. (2013, February 18). *Inventing the nation through the ballot box.* Parliament of Australia. https://www.aph.gov.au/About_Parliament/Senate/Powers_practice_n_procedures/pops/pop37/sawer

Scarfi, J. P. (2022). *Francisco de Vitoria and the (geo) politics of canonisation in Spain/America.* Leiden Journal of International Law.

Sharman, J. C. (2019). Company Sovereigns and the Empires of the East. *In Empires of the Weak: The Real Story of European Expansion and the Creation of the New World Order* (pp. 65–98). Princeton University Press.

Spiked. (2018, September 19). *Hollywood's Race War.* Spiked. https://www.spiked-online.com/2017/12/01/hollywoods-race-war/

State Library of New South Wales. (2021, March 30). *The first Indigenous Cricket tour of England in 1868.* State Library of New South Wales. https://www.sl.nsw.gov.au/stories/first-indigenous-cricket-tour-england-1868

Strachwitz, R. (2022). The Theory of the Public Sphere Revisited. *In Civil Society: Concepts, Challenges, Contexts* (pp. 31-49). Springer.

Sufi, S. (2018, July 16). *Multiculturalism has failed: Let's cut immigration, Refugee Intake.* The Australian. https://www.theaustralian.com.au/commentary/opinion/multiculturalism-has-failed-lets-cut-immigration-refugee-intake/news-story/7939b6160685f98c2fb3d6e404b6d422

Sufi, S. (2019). *The Linguistic Roots of Nationalism.* Connor Court.

Sufi, S. (2022, February 21). *115 Years of the Bondi Surf Bathers' Life Saving Club.* The Spectator Australia. https://www.spectator.com.au/2022/02/115-years-of-the-bondi-surf-bathers-life-saving-club/

Sufi, S. (2022, August 16). *Dear Lidia Thorpe, the Queen decolonised her empire like never before.* SkyNews. https://www.skynews.com.au/opinion/dear-lidia-thorpe-the-queen-is-no-coloniser-she-dissolved-her-empires-overseas-outposts-like-no-other-world-leader/news-story/209eb214df8d54f34d29a8012250934d

Sufi, S. (2022, September 12). *Don't let your guard down, the Islamist terror threat is as real as ever 21 years on from the 9/11 attacks that shocked the world.* SkyNews. https://www.skynews.com.au/world-news/dont-let-your-guard-down-the-islamist-terror-threat-is-as-real-as-ever-21-years-on-from-the-911-attacks-that-shocked-the-world/news-story/c0a6cb39a501f005f62ee008914242ab

Teo, H. M. (2021). Transported for life, transported by love: love and the Australian convict romance novel. *In The Routledge Companion to Romantic Love* (pp. 191-202). Routledge.

The Age. (2018, June 30). *Oi: No such thing as Australian values.* The Age. https://www.theage.com.au/national/oi-no-such-thing-as-australian-values-20180629-p4zojc.html

The Australian Encyclopaedia: Ferns to Ley. (1977). Grolier Society of Australia.

The British Empire in the Pacific and Australasia. (n.d.). https://

www.britishempire.co.uk/maproom/dampiersvoyages.htm

The Daily Telegraph. (2014, April 17). *Queenscliff Surf Life Saving Club proud to hear Mike Baird set to be Premier.* The Daily Telegraph. https://www.dailytelegraph.com.au/newslocal/northern-beaches/queenscliff-surf-life-saving-identity-dies/news-story/726 e9fd047fb79431b216dee7928a074

The History Press. (n.d.). *Transportation to Australia.* The History Press - The Destination for History. https://www.thehistorypress. co.uk/articles/transportation-to-australia

The Oxford Handbook of the Minor Prophets. (2021). Oxford University Press.

Tumulty, K. (2017, January 18). *How Donald Trump came up with 'Make America Great Again.'* The Washington Post. https://www.washingtonpost.com/politics/how-donald-trump-came-up-with-make-america-great-again/2017/01/17/fb6acf5e-dbf7-11e6-ad42-f3375f271c9c_story.html

United Nations. (n.d.). *Purposes and principles of the UN (Chapter I of UN Charter) Security Council.* United Nations. https://www.un.org/securitycouncil/content/purposes-and-principles-un-chapter-i-un-charter#rel2

O'Brien, J. M. (Ed.). (2021). *The Oxford Handbook of the Minor Prophets.* Oxford University Press.

The United Nations, NATO, and the Former Yugoslavia: Hearing Before the Commission on Security and Cooperation in Europe, One Hundred Fourth Congress, First Session, April 6, 1995. (1995). U.S. Government Printing Office.

The World Book Encyclopedia. (1981). World Book-Childcraft International.

Thorpe, L. (2019, January 16). *Lidia Thorpe: "Sovereignty has never been ceded".* Green Left. https://www.greenleft.org.au/content/lidia-thorpe-sovereignty-has-never-been-ceded

Vine, D. (2021). *The United States of War: A Global History of America's*

Endless Conflicts, from Columbus to the Islamic State. University of California Press.

Wang, J. (2022, January 24). *Why Australia Day has to change from January 26.* News.com.au. https://www.news.com.au/national/why-australia-day-has-to-change-from-january-26/news-story/e9cc240a65f3da20ada71ef0dfae79ca

Watson, G. (2023, June 29). *Berejiklian was right to resign, but her conduct was not criminal.* The Sydney Morning Herald. https://www.smh.com.au/politics/nsw/berejiklian-was-right-to-resign-but-her-conduct-was-not-criminal-20230628-p5dk26.html

Wild, D., Finlay, L., Sufi, S., Pawle, F., Gorman, Z., Abbott, T., Creighton, A., Foster, G., & Hussey, C. (2021). *Essays for Australia - Volume 1 2021.* Institute of Public Affairs.

Woodberry, J. (1972). *Andrew Bent and the Freedom of the Press in Van Diemen's Land.* Fullers Bookshop.

Wright, C. A. (2007). *The Medieval Spice Trade and the Diffusion of the Chile.* Gastronomica.

Yaxley, L. (2018, February 23). *Barnaby Joyce resigns as Deputy Prime Minister.* ABC News. https://www.abc.net.au/news/2018-02-23/barnaby-joyce-resigns/9477942

Yao, J. (2022). The 1815 Congress of Vienna and the oldest continuous interstate institution. *In The Ideal River* (pp. 63-83). Manchester University Press.

Zemler, E. (2023, August 4). *Critics say omitting the Japanese toll makes Oppenheimer morally half-informed.* Los Angeles Times. https://www.latimes.com/entertainment-arts/movies/story/2023-08-04/oppenheimer-movie-christopher-nolan-atomic-bomb-hiroshima-nagasaki-critics